Sustainable
LAND
MANAGEMENT

Sustainable
LAND
MANAGEMENT

Challenges, Opportunities, and Trade-offs

THE WORLD BANK
Washington, DC

ISBN-10: 0-8213-6597-5 e-ISBN: 0-8213-6598-3
ISBN-13: 978-0-8213-6597-7 DOI: 10.1596/978-0-8213-6597-7

Library of Congress Cataloging-in-Publication Data has been applied for.

CONTENTS

Tables, Figures, and Boxes   vii

Acknowledgments   ix

Acronyms and Abbreviations   xi

Overview   xiii

1. Introduction   1
2. Incidence and Effects of Land Degradation   5
   Changing Land Use: Its Causes and Implications   10
   Global Environmental Change   16
3. Challenges to Sustainable Land Management   18
   Appropriate Land Management Systems   18
   Improved Water Management   22
   Adapting to Climate Change   24
   Knowledge Dissemination and Land Policy Constraints   27
4. SLM Interventions: An Agri-technical Perspective   31
   Protecting the Land Resource: Agricultural Intensification
      and Integrated Farming Systems   34
   Soil Fertility Management   35
   Market Opportunities Linked to Erosion Control Practices:
      A Key to Adoption?   37
   Protecting and Managing Watersheds   39
   Exploiting the Production and Environmental Service Functions
      of Land   42

5. The Bank's Evolving SLM Portfolio   50
    Past and Current Investments for SLM and Related Interventions   50
    The Pattern of Bank Group Investments in SLM, NRM, BioCarbon,
        and Watershed Management Programs   51
    Lessons Learned   57

6. SLM: Strategic Options   59
    Policy and Sector Work   59
    Research and Technology Development   60
    Knowledge Sharing and Extension   63
    Providing Incentives, Expenditure Priorities, and Modes of Financing   66
    Recommended Approach and the Role of the World Bank Group   67

**Appendix: Land Management and a Useful Plant Diversity
    Index ("V" Index)   70**

Notes   73

Bibliography   75

Index   83

TABLES, FIGURES, AND BOXES

Tables

4.1 Organizing Framework for Technical Aspects of Land and Natural Resource Management at the Watershed Level   41

4.2 Economic Valuation Techniques for PES   46

5.1 Summary of SLM Strategies Implemented across Sectors   52

5.2 Selected Examples of Investments for Watershed Management Programs in Different Regions: World Bank Watershed Management Projects (1990–2004)   55

6.1 The ASB Matrix   60

Figures

2.1 The DPSIR Framework for Assessing Land Degradation and SLM Intervention Points   7

2.2 Global Food Production, Food Price, and Total Number of Undernourished People (1991–2003)   9

2.3 Agricultural Expansion and Deforestation   15

3.1 Five Broad Clusters of Forces Driving Tropical Deforestation and Land Degradation   20

4.1 Effects of Land and Water Management at the Watershed Level   40

5.1 Actual World Bank Lending by Region for Sustainable Natural Resource Management Projects with More Than 25 Percent of Total for SLM   53

5.2 BioCarbon Projects by Region   56

5.3 Carbon Value of BioCarbon Projects by Land Management Category   56

A1.1 Relationship between Land Use Type, Plant Biodiversity, and Oil Palm Tenure, Jambi, Sumatra   71

A1.2 Relationship between Land Use Type, Plant Biodiversity, and Age of Oil Palm Plantation, Jambi District, Sumatra (Indonesia)   72

A1.3 Relationship between Employment and Plant Biodiversity, Jambi, Sumatra   72

Boxes

2.1 Ecosystem Services   6

2.2 Land Use Dynamics in the Cerrado (Brazil) and the Miombo (Southern Africa)   16

3.1 Blue and Green Water Management for SLM and Enhanced Productivity   23

3.2 SLM and Enhancing Water Productivity   25

3.3 Projected Country-Level Effects of Climate Change on Rain-Fed Cereal Production (IPCC 2001)   26

4.1 A Vision for Improved Land and Water Management in Rural Landscapes   34

4.2 Linking Income-Earning and Cost-Saving Opportunities to Soil Conservation Practices and Control of Pollution and Sedimentation   39

4.3 Assessing Whether Forests and Reforestation Are Beneficial for Hydrology and Groundwater Recharge   43

4.4 Madagascar's Protected Areas and Payments for Environmental Services   48

ACKNOWLEDGMENTS

The preparation of this report was managed by the Agriculture and Rural Development (ARD) Department. Erick Fernandes and Richard Burcroff wrote the report with substantive contributions from Jonathan Anderson, Malcolm Blackie, Mustapha Ceesay, Enos Esikuri, Andrew Gillison, Nteranya Sanginga, Eric Smaling, and Erika Styger.

The authors are grateful for constructive comments and suggestions from the peer reviewers: Shawki Bhargouti, Aziz Bouzaher, Guy Evers (FAO), Nadim Khouri, James Smyle, and Mark Wilson. Many others provided inputs, including Tom Tomich (ICRAF), Steve Vosti (UC Davis), Gerhard Dieterlhe, Salah Darghouth, and Severin Kodderitzsch, as well as Melissa Williams, Marisa Baldwin, and Sarian Akibo-Betts.

Kevin Cleaver and Sushma Ganguly provided strong support throughout the development of this report and helped focus the scope of the document. The report is intended to support the efforts of the development community and national stakeholders to better integrate land and natural resource management approaches to improve rural livelihoods and reduce poverty.

ACRONYMS AND ABBREVIATIONS

ANGAP	National Association for the Management of Protected Areas in Madagascar
ASB	Alternatives to Slash and Burn
BNF	biological nitrogen fixation
CAS	country assistance strategy
CER	certified emissions reduction
CGIAR	Consultative Group on International Agricultural Research
CIMMYT	International Center for Maize and Wheat Improvement
DFID	United Kingdom Department for International Development
DPSIR	Driving Forces, Pressures, State, Impacts, Responses
ERR	economic rate of return
ESW	economic and sector work
FAO	Food and Agriculture Organization
FRP	Forestry Research Program
GDP	gross domestic product
GEF	Global Environment Facility
GIS	geographic information system
IBRD	International Bank for Reconstruction and Development
IDA	International Development Assistance
MEA	Millennium Ecosystem Assessment

NRM	natural resource management
OECD	Organisation for Economic Co-operation and Development
OED	Operations Evaluation Department
PES	payments for environmental services
PFT	plant functional type
PIR	nucleus estate/smallholder system
PRSP	poverty-reduction strategy program
SLM	sustainable land management
WSM	watershed management

OVERVIEW

In the twenty-first century, food and fiber production systems will need to meet the following three major requirements:

1. Adequately supply safe, nutritious, and sufficient food for the world's growing population.
2. Significantly reduce rural poverty by sustaining the farming-derived component of rural household incomes.
3. Reduce and reverse natural resource degradation, especially that of land.

It is now known that these challenges will need to be resolved in the face of significant but highly unpredictable changes in global climate—a key factor in natural and agroecosystem productivity. Other major issues that will influence how agriculture evolves to meet the challenge of food security include globalization of markets and trade, the increasing market orientation of agriculture, significant technological changes, and increasing public concern about the effects of unsustainable natural resource management.

The overall goal of this report is to give strategic focus to the implementation of the sustainable land management (SLM) components of the World Bank's corporate strategies. The specific objectives of the report are to articulate priorities for investment in SLM and natural resource management and to identify the policy, institutional, and incentive reform options that will accelerate the adoption of SLM productivity improvements and pro-poor growth. The primary audiences for the report are policy makers and project managers in our partner countries and development organizations, as well as Bank country and sector managers and task team leaders. There is broad interest among these partners in collaborating with the Bank on SLM and on the rehabilitation of degraded lands.

DEFINITION OF SLM

SLM is defined as a knowledge-based procedure that helps integrate land, water, biodiversity, and environmental management (including input and output externalities) to meet rising food and fiber demands while sustaining ecosystem services and livelihoods. SLM is necessary to meet the requirements of a growing population. Improper land management can lead to land degradation and a significant reduction in the productive and service (biodiversity niches, hydrology, carbon sequestration) functions of watersheds and landscapes.

In layman's terms, SLM involves:

■ Preserving and enhancing the productive capabilities of land in cropped and grazed areas—that is, upland areas, downslope areas, and flat and bottom lands; sustaining productive forest areas and potentially commercial and noncommercial forest reserves; and maintaining the integrity of watersheds for water supply and hydropower generation needs and water conservation zones and the capability of aquifers to serve farm and other productive activities.

■ Actions to stop and reverse degradation—or at least to mitigate the adverse effects of earlier misuse—which is increasingly important in the uplands and watersheds, especially those where pressure from the resident populations is severe and where the destructive consequences of upland degradation are being felt in far more densely populated areas "downstream."

CHALLENGES TO SLM

At the global level, a large area of formerly productive land has been rendered unproductive. Caution is required in interpreting the extent of land degradation and desertification described in the international literature, because local communities often have age-old strategies that allow them to manage land, forest, fallow, and water resources at variable and interacting spatial and temporal levels. However, there is a general consensus that it is far less expensive to prevent land degradation via the application of good management based on both cultural and scientific knowledge than to rehabilitate degraded land, and that where land is truly degraded, significant production and ecosystem service benefits can result from the rehabilitation of degraded lands.

The potentially deleterious effects of global climate change and natural catastrophes (earthquakes, tsunamis, hurricanes, and volcanic activity) on land resources are proving difficult to anticipate, both for the Bank and its clients and for the international community as a whole. In this area, adaptive management tailored to decrease the vulnerability of regions and communities will be increasingly necessary. Other driving forces behind degradation that can be reversed might best be termed "behavioral." These include misaligned policies and incentives; unclear property rights, especially use rights; and weak enforcement capabilities, often aggravated by corruption and governance problems.

Given the scale of potential benefits and negative effects, it is essential for problem diagnosis, assessments of resource use alternatives, and cost-benefit analyses to be conducted at appropriate spatial and temporal levels. More emphasis needs to be placed on planning and implementation at the watershed and landscape levels. Given the transboundary effects of land, water, and other resource management costs and benefits, equitable regional arrangements and treaties will need to be considered and revised as necessary.

Property rights to resources such as land, water, and trees have been found to play a fundamental role at the nexus of poverty reduction, resource management, and environmental management. The property rights held by poor people represent key household and community assets that may provide income opportunities, ensure access to essential household subsistence needs (water, food, fuel, and medicines), and insure against livelihood risk. Poorer groups tend to rely more heavily on customary or informal rights. It is unlikely that SLM can be achieved in the absence of explicit attention to property rights.

OPPORTUNITIES FOR SLM

Where land and resource management programs have been successful, the following contributing factors have often been present: (a) local community participation in all aspects of the program, (b) public support for private investment in soil and water conservation, (c) improvement and maintenance of roads, (d) sound macroeconomic management that does not discriminate against agriculture and natural resources, (e) robust local capacity building by nongovernmental organizations and other cooperative-type projects, and (f) consistent efforts over at least a decade by concerned governments to increase not only land productivity but also awareness of environmental problems and possible solutions at local levels.

Intensification of Land Use and Integrated Resource Management

Production practices that emphasize integrated nutrient and water management—for example, no-till production, conservation tillage, or mixed cropping that combines food crops with cover crop legumes and/or tree and shrub species—can greatly facilitate SLM. Coupled with enhanced management, improved breeds and varieties of animals, crops, and trees can also significantly increase resource use efficiency in agroecosystems and plantations and reduced pressure on pristine lands, including primary and healthy secondary forests.

The conservation of native above- and below-ground biodiversity is often required for sustaining ecological processes (nutrient cycles, pest-predator associations, and soil structure and function) and to maintain the resilience of most agroecosystems. The stocks of available plant nutrients need to be managed to prevent consumption from exceeding availability and, where necessary, effective recycling of crop residues and manures ought to be supplemented by external (organic and/or fertilizer) sources in order to sustain system function and productivity.

Exploiting the Production and Environmental Functions of Land

In addition to facilitating the production of food, feeds, and industrial crops, natural and agroecosystems also provide a wide variety of "nonmarket" services. The environmental benefits (or services) derived from well-managed agroecosystems typically include but are not limited to (a) improved hydrology: controlling the timing and volume of water flows and protecting water quality; (b) reduced sedimentation: avoiding damage to downstream reservoirs and waterways, thereby safeguarding uses such as hydroelectric power generation, irrigation, recreation, and providing the water necessary for fisheries and domestic water supplies; (c) disaster prevention: preventing floods and landslides; (d) biodiversity conservation; and (e) sequestering carbon and providing sinks for other greenhouse gases.

Payments for environmental services are increasingly important sources of income for land users. For example, the World Bank has pioneered the market for carbon emissions reductions via the $165 million prototype carbon fund to promote compensation for carbon emission reductions in developing countries. Communities in Central America have received payments for carbon sequestration via a program collaboratively financed by the Bank and the Global Environment Facility.

Mechanisms and Incentives for Improved Land Management at the Watershed Level

The following "best practices" have been found to facilitate upstream-downstream land and water management and the equitable assessment of costs and benefits:

- All parties in the watershed are given a stake in the management program and in watershed development functions as an equity-enhancing mechanism.
- Because water is often the most valuable resource of watershed management, it is essential to develop mechanisms that allow an equitable sharing of the water. This resource sharing can substitute for direct payments to some stakeholders.

- Where common property is involved, especially in the upper catchments, it is essential that local communities collectively protect the common land so that land and water resources are not compromised by illegal deforestation or overgrazing and subsequent land degradation.
- If irrigation water is used to produce greater vegetation biomass on common lands, biomass-sharing agreements are needed, especially for landless stakeholders.
- If water harvesting results in improved recharge of groundwater aquifers, designating groundwater as a common property resource can provide all stakeholders with a powerful incentive to improve natural resources management practices and to promote collective action.

TRADE-OFFS AND SLM STRATEGIC OPTIONS

Though the specifics will vary from country to country and region to region, there are four main components to a comprehensive strategy for facilitating sustainable land and natural resource management. These include:

- Policy and sector work
- Research and technology development
- Knowledge sharing and extension
- Providing incentives, expenditure priorities, and modes of financing

Policy and Sector Work

Further empirical work is necessary to clarify the private and social costs and benefits of alternative land use systems. Tradeoffs and synergies need to be identified and quantified where possible. Policy makers need such information when deciding on the relative priorities for the alignment of producer and consumer price incentives, fiscal and financial subsidies, licensing fees and taxation, and the structure of protection in the context of a country's environmental and social policy objectives.

Research and Technology Development

A revitalization of investments in agricultural and land use research will be needed to underpin the undertaking of SLM strategies and programs at the country and agroecological zone levels. Emphasis must be given to the adaptation and improvement of technologies associated with agricultural intensification, the management and rehabilitation of forest cover in sensitive watersheds, and more effective water management (to avert salinization and mitigate flooding) on irrigated and bottom lands.

A large number of studies have demonstrated that investments in agricultural and natural resource management research can produce significant returns. Despite this evidence, however, current trends are not encouraging. In the wake of the generally successful "Green Revolution" of the 1970s and 1980s, fiscal and financial resource transfers to most national agricultural research systems and institutes have fallen sharply. For example, African countries now spend only 0.5 percent of their agricultural gross domestic product (GDP) on research. A significantly increased adaptive effort is required on issues such as nutrient management and monitoring nutrient balances at appropriate scales, development of stress-tolerant varieties, and the rehabilitation of degraded lands.

Investing in research on how to better adapt current land management systems to cope with increasing climate variability and climate change and the associated shocks and stresses, such as drought, flood, pests, and soil salinity, will also result in improved adaptation to climate change.

Geographic information systems (GIS), geo-spatial mapping, and remote sensing technologies are central to achieving a successful transition from traditional environmental and resource management practices to sustainable development because of their integrative quality (linking social, economic, and environmental data) and their place-based quality (addressing relationships among places at local, national, regional, and global levels).

For instance, there is growing recognition by decision makers that problems at the intersection of agriculture and environmental management, climate change, and land vegetative cover change, with their attendant social and economic consequences, will be at the forefront in the new century. Technological advances in GIS fostering the integration of satellite imagery with other data (such as socioeconomic or health data) are opening new ways to synthesize complex and diverse geographic data sets, creating new opportunities for collaboration among natural and social scientists and decision makers at all levels.

Knowledge Sharing and Extension

For improved land management practices, it will be important to build farmer innovation into national extension programs and into agricultural and natural resource management initiatives. Experience shows that farmers do not passively wait for extension advice, but actively experiment and innovate with agricultural and natural resource management practices. A major advantage of innovations by farmers is that they are site-specific and often are readily acceptable to neighboring farmers. The incorporation of the farmer innovation approach within a systematic venue can significantly improve the performance of agroextension and technoadvisory services, particularly in the field of soil and water conservation, where the visual impact of demonstrations can be a powerful way to attract potential end users of new "best practices." Although land users can financially contribute to costs, public funding will be required in the poorer areas to prepare and facilitate such visits and provide follow-up. The establishment of research partnerships will be central to helping farmers conserve their land and water resources and meet other environmental and social objectives. Advising and assisting agriculturalists in this area might be commercially unattractive for private companies, but it should be an appropriate initial role for the public sector with the aim of establishing effective public-private sector partnerships.

When designing extension programs (privately operated or public sector) and the feedback systems that can capture farmer innovations, consideration should be given to establishing regional centers where information on best practices or success stories can be accessed by farmers' organizations and other entities. Such an approach is especially important in the larger countries and in those with an agroecologically diverse natural resource endowment, where a "one-size-fits-all" approach does not work and innovative technologies need to be adapted to local conditions.

Providing Incentives, Expenditure Priorities, and Modes of Financing

SLM practices are likely to be adopted where agriculture is important in rural livelihoods, where agricultural land is in short supply, and/or where SLM has the potential to increase yields of high-value crops.

Policies to facilitate SLM are more likely to be successful if they provide tangible benefits to the individual household or community by emphasizing enhanced agricultural productivity, food security, and income, rather than by controlling land degradation per se. In this context, a policy framework which provides for market access and attractive producer prices is essential to SLM.

In addition to offering policy incentives, normally operating at price and cost margins sufficient to redirect the private sector's utilization of resources in directions deemed socially desirable, achieving SLM will require additional investments in research and technology generation, knowledge dissemination, and the integration of knowledge and policies at appropriate spatial and temporal levels.

The costs of these investments can be considerable in countries where severe degradation has already taken place—often over decades and even centuries—and in those countries that will be hard hit by increasing climate variability and eventual climate change. Thus governments will need to (a) realistically assess the availability of resources, domestic and foreign, then (b) prioritize investments to rehabilitate the most egregiously damaged lands and soils (as measured, primarily, by the opportunity costs of taking no action), (c) develop a realistic phasing of investments, (d) set forth financing plans, and (e) seek agreements with likely beneficiaries in the private sector and civil society, both to participate in program implementation and to share a portion of the costs in accord with agreed mechanisms. To stimulate the involvement of private investors in land-friendly commercial activities would relieve pressures on the budget for adequate program finance while bringing to bear some of the flexibility and responsiveness needed to address the physical and financial contingencies associated with the kinds of investments mentioned. The use of risk reduction or guarantee funds or the provision of insurance, partially underwritten by government, might prove sufficient in some countries to induce a strong private sector response.

CHAPTER ONE

Introduction

This report focuses on land management issues for the sustainable intensification of food and fiber systems and for the rehabilitation of degraded crop, pasture, and forestlands. While good land management is important at the field and farm level, it is not enough to ensure sustainability. The planning and execution of sound resource management at the watershed (catchment*) level and even beyond (often referred to as the "landscape level") is increasingly important for retaining ecological integrity and ensuring that food and fiber systems are resilient enough to absorb shocks and stresses and avoid degradation of land and water resources (FRP 2005). New scientific knowledge detailing the extent and importance of ecosystem services and their roles in sustaining humans and our agroecosystems is now becoming available. The social and economic values of these services provide new opportunities for policies to encourage SLM. Recent advances in remote sensing tools will greatly facilitate the timely monitoring of land management effects and resource degradation by both users and policy makers. However, new investments will be necessary to meet the demand from land users to (a) improve access to existing knowledge and information of SLM and the consequences of inappropriate management, (b) appropriately intensify land use, and (c) rehabilitate land that has been degraded for both productive and ecosystem functions.

*The terms "watershed" and "catchment" are used interchangeably. In this context, both terms mean the topographic basin that collects water from the surrounding ridges. A landscape may contain one or more watersheds or catchments.

In the twenty-first century, food and fiber production systems will need to meet three major requirements:

1. Adequately supply safe, nutritious, and sufficient food for the world's growing population.
2. Significantly reduce rural poverty by sustaining the farming-derived component of rural household incomes.
3. Reduce and reverse natural resource degradation, especially that of land.

It is now known that these challenges will need to be resolved in the face of significant but highly unpredictable changes in global climate—a key factor in natural and agroecosystem productivity. Other major issues that will influence how agriculture evolves to meet the challenge of food security include globalization of markets and trade, the increasing market orientation of agriculture, significant technological changes, and increasing public concern about the effects of unsustainable natural resource management.

SLM is defined as a knowledge-based procedure that helps integrate land, water, biodiversity, and environmental management (including input and output externalities) to meet rising food and fiber demands while sustaining ecosystem services and livelihoods. SLM is necessary to meet the requirements of a growing population. Improper land management can lead to land degradation and a significant reduction in the productive and service functions.[1] In layman's terms, SLM involves:

- Preserving and enhancing the productive capabilities of land in cropped and grazed areas—that is, upland areas, downslope areas, and flat and bottom lands; sustaining productive forest areas and potentially commercial and noncommercial forest reserves; and maintaining the integrity of watershed for water supply and hydropower generation needs and water conservation zones and the capability of aquifers to serve the needs of farm and other productive activities.
- Actions to stop and reverse degradation—or at least to mitigate the adverse effects of earlier misuse—which is increasingly important in uplands and watersheds, especially those where pressure from the resident populations are severe and where the destructive consequences of upland degradation are being felt in far more densely populated areas "downstream."

The requisites of successful SLM do not operate in isolation from other environmentally strategic interventions. For example, SLM will clearly overlap with, and to some extent be dependent on, progress in improving the sustainability of agriculture, as well as associated soil conservation efforts; responsible water management; and accountable livestock management and reduced-impact logging practices. However, there are manifestly important aspects of

SLM that singularly pertain to the most significant land issues, namely sustaining soil productivity and averting land degradation.

The causes of the more obvious kinds of degradation have been fairly well documented. These causes—whether the result of population pressure, deforestation and abuse of forest margins, disregard (or ignorance) of the environmental consequences stemming from the dominant crop-livestock system, or industrialization and urbanization—can be grouped, in general terms, into three categories:

- Those owing to chemical and physical processes resulting from interaction between the prevailing agricultural and industrial technologies and the surrounding land resource base.
- Those of a grander or "macro" nature, such as global warming or volcanic eruption, whose consequences can be anticipated even if the onset of damage cannot be forecast with precision.
- Those whose roots are behavioral, whether deliberate—and thus the result of improper private incentives ultimately linked to market failure—or stemming from lack of knowledge or from technologies.

Not all of these causes are amenable to remediation through policy reform and institutional development, such as research, education, or reforms to "internalize the externalities" associated with land use decisions. The potentially deleterious effects of global warming and natural catastrophes (for example, earthquakes, tsunamis, hurricanes, and volcanic activity) on SLM are proving difficult to anticipate, both for the Bank and its clients and for the international community as a whole. In this area, adaptation, tailored to decrease the vulnerability of regions and communities is one viable approach. Quick fixes are not likely to show great promise, at least not from the standpoint of guaranteeing longer-term sustainability, much less a broad-based mitigation of ongoing degradation.

But much can be done to attain SLM, and it is the contention of this report that significant gains can result from understanding and respecting traditional and cultural approaches to natural resource management and generating and applying scientific and technical knowledge of the biological, chemical, and physical processes that cause or prevent degradation and desertification. Though much of the research will necessarily be tailored to local biophysical environments, such research is still needed in many parts of the world to enable us to better understand the untoward side effects of local land use practices and to establish a firmer empirical basis for improved land management. Other driving forces behind degradation that can be reversed might best be termed "behavioral." These include misaligned incentives policies; unclear property rights, especially use rights; and weak enforcement capabilities, often aggravated by corruption and governance problems. These range from (a) the most obvious misalignments between private and social costs, often encouraged through subsidies and taxes, direct and indirect, that might, for example, promote a damaging overapplication of farm chemicals or irrigation water to (b) the problem of the commons on upland rangelands, where individual property rights are unclear and the local communities' rights to regulate land use are either unclear or unenforceable to (c) the widespread and often illegal harvesting of publicly owned forestlands. All are amenable to policy reform and corrective action.

Simple lack of knowledge is another leading cause of misuse of the land resource, both by farmers and others exercising their land usufruct and by public authorities responsible for, among other things, misguided or overly expensive infrastructure construction programs, including those that prove too costly to maintain.[2] Again, such lack of knowledge, though pervasive, can be countered by education programs, as well as by technical advice and by an improvement in land use–monitoring capabilities.

The remainder of this study is presented in five chapters. Chapter 2 will review the factors underlying land degradation in some detail, including its apparent root causes and other contributing factors. In Chapter 3, the report identifies the requisites for shifting to a posture of SLM as quickly as possible in various parts of the world, and anticipates activities that should be undertaken by the international community, and especially by the Bank's client states. Chapter 4 examines in greater detail the kinds of SLM interventions likely to result in improved management and the cessation of degradation, while Chapter 5 reviews the Bank's evolving SLM portfolio. Chapter 6 then proposes an action program for the Bank.

The overall goal of this report is to highlight the key SLM issues and emerging challenges that require urgent investments and to give strategic focus to implementation of the SLM components of the World Bank's corporate strategies. Its specific objectives are to identify the policy, institutional, and incentive reform options that will accelerate the adoption of SLM productivity improvements and pro-poor growth and to articulate priorities for investment in SLM and natural resource management (NRM). The primary audiences for the report are policy makers and project managers in our partner countries and development organizations, as well as Bank country and sector managers and task team leaders. There is broad interest among these partners in collaborating with the Bank on SLM and the rehabilitation of degraded lands. The report will be widely disseminated via the Bank, the Global Environment Facility (GEF), and the United Nations Convention to Combat Desertification channels and will be used to guide external agencies and the Bank's partners on the best policy, institutional, and investment options for SLM and NRM in general.

CHAPTER TWO

Incidence and Effects of Land Degradation

At present, land use practices in many developing countries are result-ing in land, water, and forest degradation, with significant repercus-sions for the countries' agriculture sectors, natural resource bases, and ecoenvironmental balances. Land degradation can be defined as the loss of land productivity through one or more processes, such as reduced soil biolog-ical diversity and activity, the loss of soil structure, soil removal due to wind and water erosion, acidification, salinization, waterlogging, soil nutrient min-ing, and pollution.

Land degradation also results in the loss of ecosystem services (box 2.1), which further undermines the sustainability of both managed and natural ecosystems. Blaikie and Brookfield (1987) observed that land and water degra-dation may be unintentional and unperceived; it may result from carelessness or from the unavoidable struggle of vulnerable populations for the necessities of survival.

Land degradation is a global phenomenon that endangers the livelihoods of rural farmers—indeed, of the population at large—as well as a country's abil-ity to produce crops, livestock, and products from other natural resources. Population pressure, disparities in access to the more productive lands, and civil strife have all pushed farmers into cultivating ever-steeper slopes for small-scale food crop production. For example, in many African, Central American, and Southeast Asian countries 50 to 70 percent of total agricultural output value comes from hillside farms, a semi-subsistence regime whose prac-titioners are among the smallest and poorest farming households. Farming on

An ecosystem is a dynamic complex of plant, animal, and microorganism communities and the nonliving environment interacting as a functional unit. Examples of ecosystems include natural forests, landscapes with mixed patterns of human use, and ecosystems intensively managed and modified by humans, such as agricultural lands and urban areas. Ecosystem services are the benefits people obtain from ecosystems. These include:

- *Provisioning services* that provide necessities such as food, water, timber, and fiber
- *Regulating services* that affect climate, floods, disease, wastes, and water quality
- *Cultural services* that provide recreational, aesthetic, and spiritual benefits
- *Supporting services* such as soil formation, photosynthesis, and nutrient cycling

The human species, while buffered against environmental changes by culture and technology, is fundamentally dependent on the flow of ecosystem services.

Source: Millennium Ecosystem Assessment 2005.

sloping lands is difficult and the soils are more prone to erosion and degradation than on level land. In many regions, deforestation of hillsides and mountains coupled with increasing soil tillage has led to increased land degradation, soil erosion, and in some cases, landslides.

Programs, incentives, and expenditures to mitigate the factors causing land degradation and reverse its more harmful manifestations are important components of SLM.

Land degradation may result from policies that distort input markets (land, labor, capital, fertilizer, and machinery) or output markets (agriculture versus other land uses and relative crop prices). Although farmers use a variety of means to maintain the productivity of their lands, land degradation may occur where there is a disparity between private and social costs or when public policy results in less than optimal soil management. Factors such as insecure tenure, extreme poverty, and lack of access to credit often result in inadequate investment in maintaining soil capital.

The model based on Driving Forces, Pressures, State, Impacts, Responses (DPSIR) that was developed for the Organisation for Economic Co-operation and Development (OECD 1993) has been adopted as a framework and policy tool to identify management options for a range of environmental problems. The model captures the driving forces and pressures—largely controlled by human activity—and their effects on the environmental system and the state of natural resources (figure 2.1). The DPSIR model is useful for evaluating the seriousness of land degradation, as well as for identifying potential SLM intervention points, and it is currently being used by the multinational Land Degradation Assessment in Drylands project of the Food and Agriculture Organization (FAO), GEF, and the United Nations Environment Program (UNEP) (FAO 2005).

Some of the effects of poor land use practices are felt by land users themselves in the form of declining agricultural yields and higher costs to maintain current production levels. It is estimated that land degradation affects approximately 50 percent of agricultural lands on moderate slopes and 80 percent of lands on steep slopes, and that approximately 25 percent of farm households suffer significant soil losses each year (World Bank 1997). While land users often face constraints in addressing land degradation in their fields, it is somewhat reassuring that over half the farms on moderate and steeper slopes have some form of soil conservation (World Bank 1997).

Figure 2.1   The DPSIR Framework for Assessing Land Degradation and SLM Intervention Points

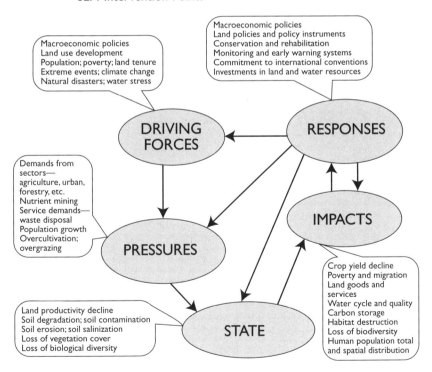

Source: OECD 1993.

Desertification is a reflection of land degradation in arid, semiarid, and dry, subhumid areas (drylands) resulting mainly from adverse human effects. It is a widespread but spatially concentrated process of land degradation in the world's drylands that is quite different from the phenomenon of observed cyclic oscillations of vegetation productivity at desert fringes (desert expansion or contraction), such as has recently been revealed by satellite data and is related to climate fluctuations. Some estimates claim that desertification directly affects about 3.6 billion hectares—70 percent of the earth's total, drylands, or nearly a quarter of its total land area. The immediate consequences of desertification are felt by about one-sixth of the world's population. These figures exclude natural hyperarid deserts.

At present, desertification in the drylands manifests itself through:

- Overexploitation and degradation of 3,333 million hectares or about 73 percent of the total area of rangelands, which are of low potential for human and animal carrying capacity and have a low population density but may be intrinsically resilient and might have considerable capacity to recuperate and regain their potential productivity if properly managed.
- Reductions in soil fertility and soil structure, leading gradually to soil loss on 216 million hectares of rain-fed croplands or nearly 47 percent of their total area in the drylands. These constitute the most vulnerable and fragile among the marginally cultivable lands subjected to increasing population pressure.
- Degradation of 43 million hectares of irrigated croplands, or nearly 30 percent of their total area in the drylands, which usually have the highest agricultural potential and the greatest population densities when well managed. (UNEP 2006)

It is important to point out, however, that there is significant uncertainty as to the true extent of degraded lands at regional and global levels (Reij et al. 1996). Nevertheless, the local, regional, and global consequences of land degradation are serious and reasonably well known. Figure 2.1 demonstrates the multiple points of potential intervention for land degradation control. Soil conservation may be the most immediate, but equally effective could be measures to stem biodiversity loss, such as reduced grazing pressure, increased water use efficiency, and protection of soil carbon stocks.

Extensive degradation also stems from the overexploitation of lands in the watersheds. When coupled with inadequate water management downstream, the consequences can be quite severe, including:

- A markedly increased vulnerability to flooding and landslides
- Dry season water scarcity
- Declining water quality from increased sediments and nutrients such as nitrogen

- Sedimentation and increased costs to hydroelectric, irrigation, and municipal water systems
- Reduced productivity of inland aquaculture and harm to marine fisheries
- Increased stress, and ultimately permanent damage, to watersheds and wetlands

Fortunately, in the past four decades, scientific advances and the application of improved knowledge and technologies by some farmers have resulted in significant total and per capita food increases, reduced food prices (figure 2.2), and the sparing of new land that otherwise would have been needed to achieve the same level of production (Evenson and Gollin 2003).

For example, if yields of the six major crop groups that are cultivated on 80 percent of the total cultivated land area had remained at 1961 levels, an additional 1.4 billion hectares of farm land—more than double the amount of land currently being used—would have been required by 2004 to serve an expanding population. Asia alone would have required an additional 600 million

Figure 2.2　Global Food Production, Food Price, and Total Number of Undernourished People (1991–2003)

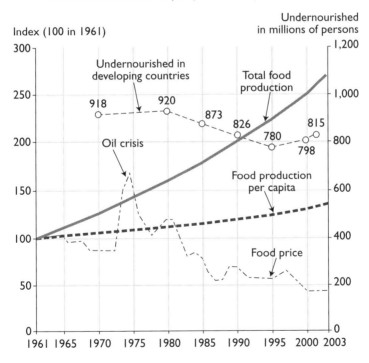

Sources: FAOSTAT 2004, SOFI 2004, Gewin 2002.

hectares, which represents 25 percent more land area than is suitable for cultivation on that continent. Rather than enjoying surpluses of grains, Asia would now be heavily dependent on food imports if crop yields had remained at 1961 levels (Wood 2005).

Although agricultural growth in Africa has been significantly lower than in Asia and Latin America, examples of quantifiable success in agriculture and SLM have also been documented. Gabre-Madhin and Haggblade (2004) identified major commodity-specific successes, such as breakthroughs in maize breeding across Africa, sustained gains in cassava breeding and control of major pests and plant diseases, successful control of the rinderpest livestock disease, booming horticultural and flower exports in East and Southern Africa, and increased cotton production and exports in West Africa. Improved land management led to higher crop yields, often derived from improved fallow management, rotations with leguminous food and cover crop species, the targeted use of rock phosphate to enhance biological, nitrogen fixation, conservation (minimum tillage) farming, and innovative livelihood diversification approaches involving agriculture and community-based wildlife management. In a study focusing on African drylands, SLM successes were found to include reforestation of degraded lands, harnessing of indigenous knowledge about soil and water conservation, and area development via the rehabilitation of degraded lands (Reij and Steeds 2003).

Despite the impressive gains in agricultural productivity via crop intensification in most regions, two negative trends persist. The first relates to the measured land degradation on some intensively cropped lands, the overuse of ground water, excessive nutrient loads in surface and ground water, and increased pesticide use. The second is the continuing expansion of agriculture into existing savanna and forest ecosystems, which often results in negative effects on ecosystem functions (for example, hydrology and predator-pest equilibria) and environmental services (greenhouse gas sinks and biodiversity refugia).[3] Both are increasingly important for sustaining rural livelihoods in the face of population pressure and encroachment.

CHANGING LAND USE: ITS CAUSES AND IMPLICATIONS

There is an emerging consensus that several, interrelated forces drive land management dynamics.

Growing Demand for Food and Fiber

The world's population is projected to reach 9 billion in 2050, and the increase will be largely in developing countries. Urban populations in developing countries will also increase, resulting in major supply issues for food and fiber, because although rural populations purchase about 40 percent of their food (approximately 60 percent comes from their fields and forests), urban populations depend on markets for close to 90 percent of their food supply. Rural-to-urban migration thus implies a twofold increase in the commercial demand for food and fiber from rural areas. Furthermore, recent changes in the nature of food demand show that a rise in incomes tends to be accompanied by a change in the nature of food demand, with a significant increase in demand for meat products. Far more natural resources are required to produce 1 kilogram of meat than 1 kilogram of grain.

Despite rapid urbanization, it will be another 10–15 years before urban and rural populations equalize. Most of the 825 million undernourished people in the world today live in the tropics. In many tropical countries, 40–70 percent of the population still lives in rural areas. Unlike relatively homogenous temperate farming systems, however, tropical systems are highly diverse and largely dominated by small-scale production systems (except in the Cerrado zone of central Brazil). Significant increases in grain production have in some cases been achieved at the expense of the natural resource base (e.g., reduced natural forest area and pollution of surface and ground water). Although complex by their very nature, mixed-food, livestock, and tree-based systems have in many cases played a vital role in sustaining rural agroecosystems and protecting the natural resources required for more homogenous grain crop systems. These systems are increasingly being neglected or converted. Managing these heterogeneous tropical landscapes involves assessing a range of land, water, biodiversity, and ecosystem service synergies and trade-offs and is challenging.

The major findings of the recently concluded Millennium Ecosystem Assessment warned that approximately 60 percent of the ecosystem supporting life on Earth was being degraded or used unsustainably and that the consequences of degradation could grow significantly worse in the next half century (MEA 2005a).

Economic Forces and Land Management Incentives

The Millennium Development Goals specifically target the reduction of poverty. Reardon and Vosti's (1995) typology of poverty is explicitly linked to the environment and the sustainable management of land and natural resources. These authors examine the asset portfolio of the rural poor in terms of

- Natural resources, such as water, ground cover, biodiversity of wild and domestic fauna and flora, and soil
- Human resources, such as education, health, nutrition, skills, and number of people
- On-farm resources, such as livestock, farmland, pastures, reservoirs, buildings, equipment, and financial resources
- Off-farm resources, including local off-farm physical and financial capital

- Community-owned resources, such as roads, dams, and commons
- Social and political capital

Where markets are absent, underdeveloped, or constrained, asset-specific poverty can influence livelihood activities and investment decisions. Many households that are not considered poor according to the usual consumption-oriented definition may have a food surplus above the minimum diet line that is still too small to make key conservation or land intensification investments necessary to prevent land and resource degradation. In some cases, such households may start cultivating highly marginal lands (conservation-investment poverty).

Land management options are strongly governed by regulatory and incentives policies, as well as public expenditure priorities. In most countries, these policies and priorities aim to improve access to and the availability of raw materials. Included, for example, are infrastructure development incentives and public expenditures (for access roads, water control facilities, and the like) and land use or land management policies allowing for such things as resource extraction, logging, oil exploration, and urbanization.

These types of policies can either be supportive of or run counter to sustainable resource management, especially with respect to environmental and social goals. Identifying perverse incentives and underlying economic forces that lead to resource degradation is critical for SLM, a key element of which must be implementation of the kinds of incentives that will lead to more efficient land management and optimal output levels.

In practice, the following types of incentives are commonly applied:

- *Policy-Related Incentives.* Generally, policies to stimulate sectoral development—often in the form of direct inducements—are employed in conjunction with taxes, subsidies, and new laws. Such policies can result in land degradation when they encourage a particular form of land use that excludes other options (for example, monoculture versus mixed cropping and the planting of annual crops versus perennials), when they promote human settlements in ecologically sensitive areas (with, for example, the draining of wetlands or clearing of native forests for agriculture in catchments), or when they fail to account for waste management and nonpoint source pollution.
- *Market-Based Incentives.* The price mechanism strongly influences the relative profitability of land management options, and thus land user decisions on production and consumption levels. If markets are inefficient and prices are distorted, land and other natural resource endowments may be significantly undervalued, leading to overconsumption and resource degradation. Thus, artificially low royalties and stumpage fees in forestry, cheap fertilizers and pesticides, and lack of environmental service markets can result in land degradation.

■ *Institutional Arrangements.* Institutions set and control the terms and conditions under which natural resources are managed, allocated, and used. Both local and national-level institutions affect natural resource use. Land degradation can result when local or national institutions favor the interests of a particular group of land users over other users, when local communities are excluded from decision making and participation in management and benefits, and when land and resource tenure arrangements are left unresolved.

Beyond interventions and actions by government and various stakeholders, the conditions on the ground also impact land use choices. The most vulnerable communities are usually in marginal areas that are likely to be further affected by changing global climate. Widespread poverty and the lack of livelihood options usually lead to resource mining and degradation. Poor infrastructure and lack of markets lock subsistence communities, in particular, in a downward spiral of unsustainable resource extraction and degradation. There are encouraging examples of how policy-driven, science-based land use intensification can deflect pressure from pristine areas (Binswanger et al. 1987; Deininger and Minten 1996). In the Philippines and Vietnam, for example, the adoption of lowland rice intensification technologies appears to have attracted labor from upper watersheds, thereby reducing deforestation (Muller and Zeller 2002; Shively and Pagiola 2004). In the absence of adequate policies and regulatory frameworks, however, improved technologies and or mechanization can lead to higher agricultural productivity and may fuel deforestation (Angelsen and Kaimowitz 2001; Pichon 1997), for example, soybean expansion in the *cerrado* and pastures in the Amazon forest.

Agricultural Intensification in Rain-Fed and Irrigated Systems

Sustainable land and natural resource management is fundamental to ensuring adequate food and fiber production. A sustainable and increasingly productive agricultural base is essential for global food security. Farmers use close to 70 percent of the world's arable and rangelands, and fresh water supplies and are constantly influencing the boundaries of the remaining pristine areas (forests, wetlands, and coasts) on the planet.

In a review of resources and projections for global food prospects to 2030, Crosson and Anderson (1993) highlighted the following as important for sustaining agricultural productivity.

■ Land quality is an important issue among the long-run considerations related to global food supply.
■ The total potential supply of additional cropland will be substantially less than the current supply of farmland.

- The contribution of increased irrigation water to agricultural production in selected countries will be sizeable, but global supplies of irrigation water will be increasingly constrained.
- New and more productive varieties of food and other crops developed via advances in accessing genetic material from wild relatives and plant breeding are likely to contribute to enhanced food supplies.
- Climate variability will continue, but neither detract from nor enhance food production possibilities.
- Property rights—clearly specified, well defined, and enforceable—are quite important in facilitating good resource management directly or via appropriate policies and incentives.
- Based on previous yield improvements in cereals and reductions in environmental costs of agriculture, and anticipating major breakthroughs in disease resistance and crop yield potentials, food supplies will be adequate to meet demand.

In the past two decades, more than 70 percent of the increased cereal production in Sub-Saharan Africa is estimated to have resulted from crop area expansion, whereas other regions have achieved 80 percent of their increased production via yield increases (FAO 2000; Dorward et al. 2004). The current hotspots of deforestation for subsistence and plantation crops are in the Congo and Indonesia, and for ranching and settlement in the Amazon (figure 2.3). Addressing the land management problems associated with areal expansion in Africa is a priority, because it is resulting in land degradation at a comparatively faster rate than in the other Bank regions.[4] The most severe incidence of degradation is being felt in Africa's forest and woodland and in that continent's savanna-ecosystem services (Scholes and Biggs 2004). Current evidence suggests that climate variability and medium- to long-term climate change are likely to significantly increase the risk of crop failures due to factors such as drought, flood, expanding pest and pathogen ranges, and increased competition from aggressive and better-adapted invasive weeds.

Although it is estimated that there are probably around 1.8 billion hectares of potential agricultural land still available, mainly in Latin America and Sub-Saharan Africa, significant soil and other biophysical constraints will limit the projected expansion of cultivated lands to around 120 million additional hectares. The likely zones for significant further crop and livestock area expansion, at significant cost to biodiversity and ecosystem services, are the Cerrado zone in Brazil and the Miombo zone in southern Africa (see box 2.2).

Despite the impressive increases in agricultural productivity over the past four decades, continuing expansion of agricultural areas, coupled with increasing production risks from climate variability and the negative effects of past land management on ecosystem services, suggests an increased urgency for sustainable productivity gains on existing crop-, pasture-, and forestlands.

Figure 2.3　Agricultural Expansion and Deforestation

Source: MEA 2005a.

Box 2.2 Land Use Dynamics in the Cerrado (Brazil) and the Miombo (Southern Africa)

The Cerrado zone covers 1.8 million square kilometers in central Brazil, Paraguay, and Bolivia, with around 80 percent of the area already converted to agriculture or modified in a major way (Mittermeier et al. 1999). The region is important for its biodiversity, for its capacity for carbon storage, and as South America's most important watershed (three major basins have sources here— the Paraná, the Amazon, and the São Francisco). The Pantanal, surrounded by *cerrado,* is one of the world's most biologically rich wetlands. The current expansion of intensive soybean cultivation in the Cerrado zone of Brazil is largely displacing poorly productive or degraded pastures, although new clearings of the original vegetation are also occurring. Furthermore, there are reports of nutrient loading and pesticide pollution from some of the intensive high-input agricultural systems (such as that for cotton) and the displacement of small farmers by large-scale soybean farmers and beef ranchers.

In southern Africa, the Miombo woodland savanna zone stretches across seven eastern, central, and southern African countries (Angola, the Democratic Republic of Congo, Malawi, Mozambique, Tanzania, Zambia, and Zimbabwe). The woodlands cover an area of about 2.7 million square kilometers and sustain a population of about 40 million people (Desanker et al. 1997). The *miombo* woodlands are also quite important from a biodiversity perspective, with more than half of their 8,500 plant species found nowhere else on earth (WWF 2001), and have traditionally been managed by local people for a large variety of food, timber, and nontimber forest products (Dewees 1996). Scholes (1996) suggests that the increasing demand for food may result in unsustainable clearing of the *miombo.*

Given some of the similarities in the biophysical factors of the Miombo zone in southern Africa to the Cerrado zone in Brazil, agricultural intensification there is also likely to be an increasing focus on some parts of the *miombo* for intensification of cereal cropping. The positive and negative lessons of agricultural expansion in the *cerrado,* coupled with state-of-the-art remote sensing and resource monitoring and evaluation tools, can help the targeted development of intensive grain cropping systems on already cleared farmland in the *miombo* and prevent most of the problems of resource degradation that occurred in the early days of agronomic intensification in the *cerrado.*

GLOBAL ENVIRONMENTAL CHANGE

Based on a range of scenarios, the Millennium Ecosystem Assessment (MEA 2005a) projections (with a medium to high level of certainty) show that land use change, primarily associated with the expansion of agriculture, will remain the dominant driver of change in terrestrial and fresh-water ecosystems. An additional driver, closely coupled with land management and intensive agriculture, is nutrient loading, which already has major adverse effects on fresh-water ecosystems and coastal regions in both industrial and developing countries. The major nutrient in question is nitrogen. Three out of four scenarios project (with a medium level of certainty) that global fluxes of nitrogen in coastal ecosystems will increase by 10–20 percent until 2030. The effects of nutrient loading include toxic algae blooms, other human health problems, fish kills, and damage to habitats such as coral reefs. The amount of river nitrogen will not change in most industrial countries, while a 20–30 percent increase is projected for developing countries, particularly in Asia.

A key question is this: To what extent can good land management contribute to sustaining a high level of agricultural productivity in intensive mono-culture and mixed crop–, livestock-, and tree-based systems and maintain environmental services? Integrated soil, nutrient, and water conservation approaches that combine technologies based on biological, chemical, and physical principles could significantly reduce the negative externalities of intensive crop and livestock systems and improve the productivity of lower-yielding but environmentally friendly production systems in more marginal farming areas.

Because preventing land degradation is usually far less expensive and more effective than rehabilitating badly degraded lands, the first priority is to prevent the degradation of currently productive land. The second priority is to rehabilitate moderately degraded lands and then the severely degraded lands via measures that facilitate the recovery of soil biological communities essential to efficient nutrient conservation and soil physical integrity (Uphoff et al. 2006), improve the nutrient status via added fertilizer nutrients if necessary, and increase the amount of organic carbon in soil. Clearly, however, local community and government priorities should take precedence when deciding what needs to be done in any particular location.

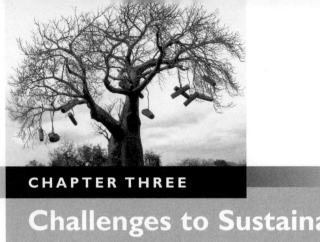

CHAPTER THREE

Challenges to Sustainable Land Management

A significant land management paradigm change in recent years involves assessment of the impacts of management of land and water at field levels on the larger watershed (catchment) and even landscape. Because agroecological landscapes are diverse, farmers and land users have developed a broad set of cropping and natural resource management strategies to cope with the diversity of production and ecological conditions. Adequate treatment of the complexity of agroecological conditions and cropping systems is beyond the scope of this report. Refer to the comprehensive work *Farming Systems and Poverty* by Dixon et al. (2001) for more information.

APPROPRIATE LAND MANAGEMENT SYSTEMS

Five broad pathways of agricultural land use change have evolved in developing countries in this century, reflecting different land resource endowments and settlement patterns:

- Expansion and intensification of irrigated agriculture
- Intensification of high-quality rain-fed lands
- Intensification of densely populated marginal lands
- Expansion of farming into sparsely populated marginal lands
- The rise of urban and periurban farming with accelerated urbanization

Agricultural landscapes in the five pathways are typically quite distinct, and they offer quite different risks of resource degradation and opportunities and constraints for intensification, diversification, and land-improving investment. Further landscape differences and resource management challenges arise from variations in the land's settlement history and its past history of degradation; the mix of crop, perennial, and livestock components; and the mix of commercial and subsistence enterprises. For example, Templeton and Scherr (1997) found empirical evidence that the relationship between population growth and resource quality on hills and mountains was influenced by rainfall (mainly by affecting crop-product choice, risks of soil degradation, and land use intensity), topography (by affecting the spatial distribution of production systems), and soil characteristics (through crop choice, cropping frequency, and input use). These factors also affected returns to conservation.

A review by Geist and Lambin (2002) has provided a framework for analyzing and classifying the causes of deforestation, and potentially land degradation (figure 3.1). These authors examined and compared the factors at work in 152 cases of tropical deforestation in Africa, Asia, and Latin America. They distinguish between the proximate causes of deforestation—human activities on the ground at the local level—and the larger driving forces that underlie these activities. In their analytical framework, four broad clusters of proximate causes—agricultural expansion, wood extraction, infrastructure development, and other factors—are linked to five clusters of underlying causes: demographic, economic, technological, policy and institutional, and cultural. In each case, the clusters are subdivided into more specific factors. For example, agricultural expansion may take the form of permanent cultivation, shifting cultivation, cattle ranching, or colonization (see figure 3.1).

A mix of causes is normally at work when deforestation occurs. The review goes on to identify what it calls "causal synergies"—associations of proximate and underlying causes that help to explain deforestation more convincingly than previous "single-factor" explanations. Together with other recent research, the review by Geist and Lambin (2002) tells us much about the real and often complex interacting causes of tropical deforestation.

Although agricultural expansion was found to be at least one of the factors in 96 percent of the cases, shifting cultivation of food crops by smallholders, so often thought to be a major cause, was in fact a relatively minor contributor to deforestation. Other forms of agricultural expansion, such as permanent cropping or cattle ranching, appear equally or more significant in most regions, though the agroecological and policy factors influencing this cause of forest loss vary considerably across regions—with very different pathways identified for the Amazon, the Congo Basin, and Southeast Asia—and even within regions across countries.

Far more influential than shifting cultivation, or indeed any of the proximate causes of deforestation, are the macroeconomic forces that create the incentives to which individuals respond. Often these forces manifest themselves as shocks that destabilize the lives of poor people, for example, a massive increase in urban unemployment triggering reverse migration into the countryside. These shocks punctuate longer periods in which social and economic

Figure 3.1 Five Broad Clusters of Forces Driving Tropical Deforestation and Land Degradation

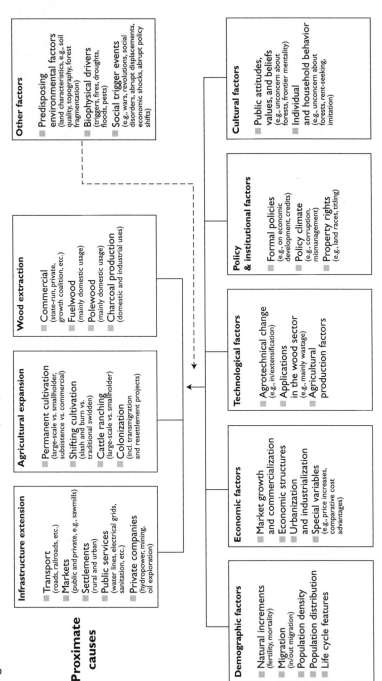

Proximate causes

Infrastructure extension
- Transport (roads, railroads, etc.)
- Markets (public and private, e.g., sawmills)
- Settlements (rural and urban)
- Public services (water lines, electrical grids, sanitation, etc.)
- Private companies (hydropower, mining, oil exploration)

Agricultural expansion
- Permanent cultivation (large-scale vs. smallholder, subsistence vs. commercial)
- Shifting cultivation (slash and burn vs. traditional swidden)
- Cattle ranching (large-scale vs. smallholder)
- Colonization (incl. transmigration and resettlement projects)

Wood extraction
- Commercial (state-run, private, growth coalition, etc.)
- Fuelwood (mainly domestic usage)
- Polewood (mainly domestic usage)
- Charcoal production (domestic and industrial uses)

Other factors
- Predisposing environmental factors (land characteristics, e.g., soil quality, topography, forest fragmentation)
- Biophysical drivers (triggers, fires, droughts, floods, pests)
- Social trigger events (e.g., wars, revolutions, social disorders, abrupt displacements, economic shocks, abrupt policy shifts)

Underlying causes

Demographic factors
- Natural increments (fertility, mortality)
- Migration (in/out migration)
- Population density
- Population distribution
- Life cycle features

Economic factors
- Market growth and commercialization
- Economic structures
- Urbanization and industrialization
- Special variables (e.g., price increases, comparative cost advantages)

Technological factors
- Agrotechnical change (e.g., in/extensification)
- Applications in the wood sector (e.g., mainly wastage)
- Agricultural production factors

Policy & institutional factors
- Formal policies (e.g., on economic development, credits)
- Policy climate (e.g., corruption, mismanagement)
- Property rights (e.g., land races, titling)

Cultural factors
- Public attitudes, values, and beliefs (e.g., unconcern about forests, frontier mentality)
- Individual and household behavior (e.g., unconcern about forests, rent-seeking, imitation)

Source: Geist and Lambin 2002.

trends bring about more gradual changes in the opportunities available to poor rural people, such as the steady growth of the international timber trade or of the demand for livestock products and the steadily expanding ecological and economic "footprint" of distant city markets. The economic integration of forest margins and the continual development of product and labor markets that accompany this process are factors at work in almost all cases.

Strongly associated with the influence of macroeconomic forces is the building of roads. Often paid for by logging companies or through international aid, new roads open up forest areas, first for wood extraction and then for the expansion of agriculture. New migrants colonize roadsides and use roads to obtain inputs and deliver their produce to markets. By linking forested areas to the broader economy, roads lower costs and increase the returns of conversion, heightening the sensitivity of these areas to changes in macroeconomic conditions.

In this report, we highlight the low- to moderate-input systems that optimize nutrient recycling—via residue return, conservation tillage, soil conservation, and protection of riparian zones—as the recommended baseline upon which to build production systems that may require the increasing use of external inputs. For example, the use of efficient biological nitrogen fixation (BNF) technology by Brazilian soybean farmers results in approximately US$ 200 million annual savings from not using nitrogen fertilizers. Given the fact that the nitrogen use efficiency of fertilizer rarely exceeds 30 percent and excess nitrates can either contaminate ground water or be denitrified to produce nitrous oxide—a greenhouse gas 310 times more powerful than carbon dioxide—BNF contributions to high levels of soybean productivity also result in significant environmental benefits.

Land users can foster a variety of environmental services, ranging from regulation of hydrological flows to biodiversity conservation and carbon sequestration. However, land uses that provide such services are rapidly being displaced by uses that do not. A key reason is that land users typically receive no compensation for environmental services they generate for others.

As an example, the link between agricultural practices on hillsides and environmental degradation has clear implications for land use: farmers must be induced to adopt sustainable agricultural systems that favor the production of environmental services while also allowing them to increase their food security and incomes.

Land degradation and its relation to rural poverty remain poorly understood, though the link remains very much in evidence. A downward spiral of land degradation and poverty may be occurring—a kind of physical-technical equivalent to the Lewis low-income trap—with land degradation causing declining agricultural productivity and worsening poverty, and poverty causing households to further degrade their land.

More recently, soil conservation measures have relied largely on food-for-work programs as an incentive and have been oriented toward labor-intensive activities such as terracing, bund construction, and tree planting. There is a growing consensus that the effects of past soil conservation programs have been rather disappointing (Bojo 1996; Bekele and Holden 1999), although there is evidence of positive effects from conservation measures in some areas, especially within lower-rainfall regimes (Pender 2004).

The general failure of past conservation efforts can be attributed to a range of factors that make the recommended strategies inappropriate to local conditions. In particular, these have tended to focus on arresting soil erosion without considering the underlying socioeconomic causes of low soil productivity, thus promoting technologies that are not profitable or are risky or ill suited to farmers' food security needs and financial constraints (Pagiola 1999). Conservation efforts have also neglected the pronounced regional disparities within a given country and have frequently been implemented in a top-down manner, absent the participation of the local communities.

For example, research has shown that terracing and several other land management practices can increase productivity fairly quickly by increasing soil moisture retention, and thus are profitable for farmers in lower-rainfall areas of the northern Ethiopian highlands (Pender and Gebremedhin 2004). The same techniques are much less profitable in higher-rainfall areas of the highlands because they can actually reduce farmers' yields by reducing the effective area of the plot, causing waterlogging, or causing crops to harbor pests (Herweg 1993). By contrast, the use of fertilizer and improved seeds is much more profitable and less risky in higher-rainfall areas than in lower-rainfall areas, which explains the limited effect of the agricultural extension programs found in lower-rainfall areas (Pender and Gebremedhin 2004) compared to very positive effects of the programs found in higher-rainfall areas (Benin 2005).

IMPROVED WATER MANAGEMENT

Rainfall is the basic fresh-water source over a river basin. An average of 110,000 cubic kilometers of rain falls over the continents annually. Two-thirds of the rainfall is either consumed by plants or returned to the atmosphere by evaporation and transpiration (green water). Around one-third reaches the aquifers, rivers, and lakes (blue water), out of which only about 12,000 cubic kilometers is considered readily available for human use. Current water withdrawals for municipal, industrial, and agricultural use amount to some 10 percent of the blue-water resource. Green water is a very important resource for global food production. About 60 percent of the world's staple food production relies on rain-fed irrigation, hence on green water. The livestock-grazing and -browsing production systems rely on green water, as does the production of wood from natural and plantation forestry (box 3.1).

Lending for irrigation (blue water) in Sub-Saharan Africa has declined considerably over the past two decades. There are thought to be various reasons for this decline, but the common denominator is the disappointing performance

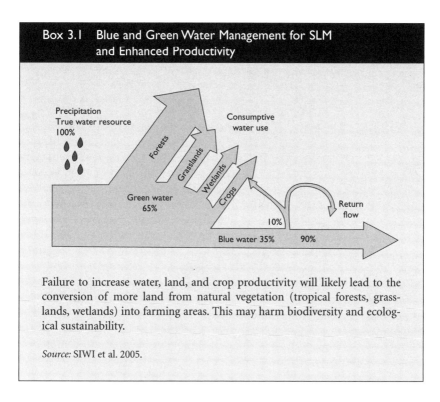

Box 3.1 Blue and Green Water Management for SLM and Enhanced Productivity

Precipitation
True water resource
100%

Consumptive
water use

Forests

Grasslands

Wetlands

Crops

Green water
65%

Return
flow

10%

Blue water 35%   90%

Failure to increase water, land, and crop productivity will likely lead to the conversion of more land from natural vegetation (tropical forests, grasslands, wetlands) into farming areas. This may harm biodiversity and ecological sustainability.

Source: SIWI et al. 2005.

of development to date in terms of sustainability and returns on investment. Moreover, the decline in irrigation lending has been matched by declining farm gate prices for food crops, further depressing returns to investment in agricultural water control facilities. That the decline in investment has continued for more than 20 years indicates that the sector has been slow to respond and adapt to change. However, if the decline in investment is to be turned around, innovative approaches to blue water, green water, and agricultural water development are now required. Refer to *Reengaging in Agricultural Water Management* (World Bank 2006b).

Although green water is the largest component of fresh-water resources, it has been neglected in policy, investment, action, and research. Green water deserves attention from policy makers, planners, land users, and investment agencies for the following reasons (Falkenmark et al. 1998):

- Rain-fed agriculture contributes most of the world's food production: 95 percent in Sub-Saharan Africa, where it makes use of only 15–30 percent of rainfall; the rest is lost, mostly as destructive runoff.
- The partitioning of rainwater into green water and blue water is a dynamic process (governed by rainfall intensity, terrain, land cover, and soil) that may be controlled by SLM approaches.

- Management of green water contributes to blue water. Soils process several times more water than they retain, while soil erosion, by runoff and bank erosion during peak flows, contributes nearly all the sediment load of streams, leading to the siltation of reservoirs and water courses.
- More effective management of green water can mitigate the competition and potential conflict between agricultural water users on the one hand and the needs of industry, urban populations, and the environment on the other.

In areas where crop, livestock, and forestry productivity is constrained by drought and recurring water deficits, supplementary irrigation from groundwater could be the key to breaking the poverty trap. Water use efficiency in drought-prone, rain-fed agriculture may be as low as 6,000 cubic meters of water consumed per ton of grain produced. A crucial question for poverty eradication, therefore, is this: How can rain-fed crop yields be improved by supplementary irrigation based on water harvested from local rainwater or flash floods and stored in small tanks? If green water was properly partitioned via water harvesting and storage, relatively small quantities of blue water (irrigation) would be required to safeguard crop and livestock production. This would result in significantly higher yields of blue water per cubic meter than can be attained from full-scale (dry season) irrigation alone. This is one reason why systems for deep-rooted tree production, which can utilize both green- and blue-water components, often function as important safety-net production systems for farmers and pastoralists in drought-prone areas.

Green water is vital for food and wood production, water supply (water tables and flows in springs and streams), water quality (including salinity and the dilution function of fresh water in wetlands), aquatic ecosystems, and waste treatment. SLM can positively affect green water, and thus significantly enhance irrigation "crop per drop" efficiency. Such innovation will also require adaptive plant research studies of crop-water relationships and of soil chemistry, structure, and permeability for many of the potential service areas (box 3.2).

ADAPTING TO CLIMATE CHANGE

Because of the certainty of global climate change, but also the extreme unpredictability of when, where, and to what extent regional and microclimates will change, a business-as-usual approach to increasing food and fiber productivity may not prove sustainable over the longer term. Climate variability is highly significant for many developing countries, especially in most of Africa (box 3.3), and it can be a major impediment to development if it is not addressed properly and managed well across a range of sectors. Unfortunately, there are few countries where climate variability is managed well today. As a consequence, improved *climate risk management* offers a low-cost opportunity for deriving greater benefit from existing land and water resources through better use of knowledge already gained.

Box 3.2   SLM and Enhancing Water Productivity

In both rain-fed and irrigated food production systems, the potential to improve water productivity—that is, to produce more food per unit of water—is substantial.

The measures required include:

■ Improved management of water in irrigated and rain-fed agriculture based on secure water use rights and land tenure.
■ Improvement of biological, chemical, and physical properties of the soil through improved land management (conservation tillage, mulching, and the construction of microcatchments).
■ Dry spell mitigation though rainwater harvesting and supplementary irrigation.
■ Effective arrangements and support services for marketing, affordable credit, technological improvements, and extension services, with a particular focus on rain-fed agriculture.
■ Investment in new irrigation and storage infrastructure and improved management of existing irrigation.

Source: SIWI et al. 2005; World Bank 2006b.

The main land-related influences of climate change will be experienced by the changing availability of agricultural water resources, its effects on attainable agricultural production and food security, and the changing requisites of natural resource management and maintenance of biodiversity. The effects of climate change will be felt in both agricultural and fisheries sectors. Changes in soil moisture and temperature, evapo-transpiration, and rainfall, and possible increases in heat stress, will affect the growth of some subsistence root crops and many open-field vegetables. Land use and the agroecology of many islands in the Pacific, the Indian Ocean, and the Caribbean, which are already experiencing water scarcity, will suffer even more from climate change. The resulting floods and droughts will also have a negative effect on agriculture. On the lowest islands—and there are many—rising sea levels will change the height of the water table and increase salinization. The viability of food crops with low salt tolerance will become a major issue (IPCC 2001).

It is likely that global warming and the resulting climate change will affect the production of certain crops, such as rice, wheat, corn, beans, and potatoes, which are major food crops for many people in Africa (IPCC 2001). Other crops, such as millet, are resistant to high temperatures and low levels of water, and so may be less affected by future climate change. An experiment in Zimbabwe showed that an increase in temperature of 2 to 4 degrees Celsius caused

Box 3.3   Projected Country-Level Effects of Climate Change on Rain-Fed Cereal Production (IPCC 2001)

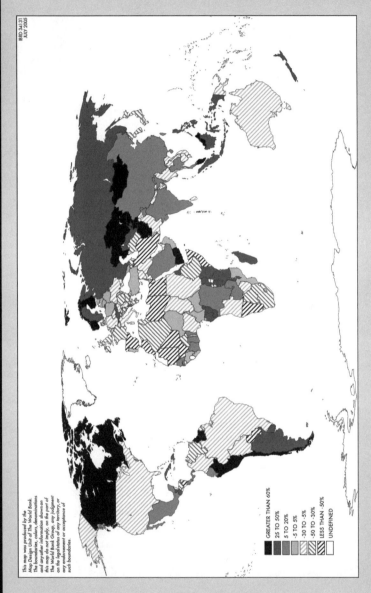

IBRD 34131
JULY 2005

GREATER THAN 60%
25 TO 50%
5 TO 20%
-5 TO 5%
-30 TO -5%
-50 TO -30%
LESS THAN -50%
UNDEFINED

The potential threat to global water and food security is severe if mean temperatures rise 1.5 to 2 degrees Celsius, with particularly disastrous consequences for the Mediterranean region and Southern Africa. The net balance of changes in food production potential for poor regions, such as Sub-Saharan Africa, will very likely be negative, with up to 12 percent of the region's current production potential lost and with as many as 40 percent of the Sub-Saharan countries losing a substantial part of their agricultural production.

a reduction of maize yield at all experimental sites. Changes in farming systems may compensate for some yield reductions, although additional inputs such as fertilizers and increased irrigation may be needed, involving extra costs to the farmers. Food-importing countries will be at greater risk, although the effects may have more to do with changes in world markets than with changes in the local climate and agricultural production (IPCC 2001).

Climate change will also affect both marine and inland fisheries. In some cases, temperature increases will increase productivity. It is projected that a warming of 3 to 5 degrees Celsius will increase the productivity of the Gambia River by about 13–21 percent. However, some fish species might be more sensitive to temperature, and increases of 3 to 4 degrees Celsius could negatively affect catfish and herring populations. On the other hand, it is estimated that shrimp yields will increase significantly (IPCC 2001). A decline in marine and aquatic fish stocks will mean that people who currently depend on fishing for food and livelihoods will turn to already depleted land resources for food production. A reduction in annual precipitation will affect the numbers of range-fed livestock in many African regions. Pastoral livelihoods in the semiarid zones of Africa are likely to be adversely affected by climate change, because several global climate models predict a decrease in mean annual precipitation of about 10–20 percent, and this will affect the dry-matter intake of pastoralists' animal herds.

To increase the adaptive capacity of rural landscapes against climate change and the expected increase in the frequency and severity of extreme events such as floods and droughts, the land management paradigm will require significant shifts of at least two types. The first is a shift in focus and perspective, from a "view from the field" (or paddock) to a broader watershed or even a landscape referent. Though highly desirable, this shift could introduce an added complexity, because it not only would encompasses a wider spatial reference, but it also would have to take into account interacting social, political (national and transnational), and economic domains. Additionally, attention will more frequently need to be given to arresting and reversing the degradation of ecosystem services and the resultant biotic and abiotic stress. Increased efforts will be required to advance scientific knowledge in general, in particular knowledge of biotechnology (that is, agronomy, genetics, pest management, and near-real-time monitoring, evaluation, and response).[6]

KNOWLEDGE DISSEMINATION AND LAND POLICY CONSTRAINTS

Low levels of land productivity and subsequent land and resource degradation can often be traced to inadequate access to the best or most appropriate knowledge required to overcome local constraints. Providing better information to both technology developers and farmers can stimulate the adoption of both soil conservation technologies and improved land management practices. For example, technology developers may lack information about cropping patterns and practices that might serve the priorities of farmers and at the same time contribute to soil conservation. This information could be used to focus technology development efforts.

Farmers are usually aware when degradation threatens their immediate livelihoods. When a lack of concern is shown, it is often because farmers either have not yet considered degradation a serious longer-term threat or because the resource in question provides only a marginal contribution to farm family livelihoods (Scherr and Hazell 1994; Enters 1998).

In several situations, however, lack of farmer awareness significantly constrains adaptation. The first is when degradation effects, or their causal factors, are not immediately observable by farmers without modern measuring devices. Such situations may occur with soil acidification, micronutrient depletion, changes in microfauna, or spread of disease vectors.

The second is the case of recent immigrants who are farming in unfamiliar agroenvironmental conditions or are attempting to employ unfamiliar farming systems. In such instances, external intervention in problem diagnoses, farmer education, and demonstration of the positive effects of resource management change may be needed to trigger an adaptive response.

A third situation occurs when the type of resource degradation involved is not simply a local concern, but rather a concern to outsiders, as may be the case with some types of habitat loss or downstream sedimentation. An adaptive response is unlikely to be triggered without the provision of appropriate incentives, regulatory and conflict interest frameworks, and noncompliance penalties as appropriate.

A fourth situation arises when poor farmers fail to respond because of a short planning horizon or a high discount rate. The empirical evidence as to whether the poor really have high rates of time preference is sketchy, however. Furthermore, Pagiola (1995) argues that poor farmers often have an even greater willingness to protect or invest their natural resource assets than do the well-off because of their relatively greater dependence on those assets for livelihood security.

Property rights to resources such as land, water, and trees have been found to play a fundamental role in the poverty reduction–resource management–environmental management nexus. On the one hand, they govern the patterns of natural resource management and may either impede or facilitate sustainable use, protection, or resource-improving investment. On the other hand, they determine important aspects of the welfare of individuals, households, and communities who depend on those resources.

Natural resources (land, water, trees, and vegetation), rather than having a single "owner," commonly involve diverse property rights that may be held by different people, including the rights to access, withdraw, manage, or exclude others from a resource and the right to transmit or alienate rights (Schlager and Ostrom 1992). Men and women, people of different castes, local people or outsiders, and both individuals and the state may have rights to use the resource in different ways: for different crops, grazing, and gathering from land; for irrigating, washing, drinking, or other enterprises from water; and for timber, fruits, leaves, firewood, shade, or other products from trees. Property rights may be acquired through a variety of means: (a) market purchases; (b) inheritance, transfers, or gifts; (c) labor or other types of investment in improving the resource; (d) adverse possession ("squatters'" rights); (e) grants by the state; and (f) membership in a community (especially in communal or common property regimes) (Meinzen-Dick et al. 1997).

The property rights held by poor people represent key household and community assets that may provide income opportunities, ensure access to essential household subsistence needs (water, food, fuel, and medicines), and insure against livelihood risk. Poorer groups tend to rely more heavily on customary or informal rights. Marginal users, such as women and the poor, thus often lose out as a result of policies and processes that privatize and reduce complex bundles of rights into a single unitary right (under many land and water reforms) (Baland and Platteau 1996; Otsuka and Quisumbing 1998).

Property rights also affect long-term agricultural productivity and incentives for resource conservation and investment. For example, more equitable access to natural resources by women has been found not only to improve welfare outcomes for women, but also to increase agricultural productivity, the economic returns to agroforestry, and the use efficiency of water in irrigation projects (Meinzen-Dick et al. 1997). Tenure security, though not necessarily formal titling, is associated with cropland conservation practices and improvements.

Bruce and Mearns (2004) identified the importance of addressing the underlying incentive framework in ways that match the complexity and diversity of local livelihood systems rather than out of concern for sustainability that it is not shared, or is defined very differently, by the resource users themselves. Very often, external change agents must understand what else is needed to foster an enabling environment for sustainable land management (so-called tenure +), which may call for supporting interventions to improve access to alternative forms of capital (human, social, physical, and financial).

The weakness of conventional property rights approaches to NRM is well illustrated in pastoral systems in which an important goal is to achieve sustainability by balancing the number of grazing livestock against the long-run carrying capacity of the range. A common assumption of outsiders is that pastoralists are unable to control access to and use of resources among their members. So it is taken for granted that the appropriate management solution is to assign property rights to individuals (or to the state). Given the high level of ecological variability and risk, however, livestock producers in such systems need to be able to "track" available forage or browse for their livestock, which usually requires that they have access to large areas that encompass a diverse range of upland ecological niches. Small-scale subdivisions and property rights can greatly reduce the opportunistic tracking strategies needed to cope with resource variability, and thereby increase vulnerability, overgrazing, and land degradation and conflicts.

While monitoring and evaluation methodologies are well established, there cannot be a universal approach to monitoring, for instance, by relying on a single pre-established set of indicators, however comprehensive and encompassing these might be. Rather, a balance among the previously described features must be struck and tailored to the unique set of agroecological environments, as well as to the discrete specifics of the programs, interventions, and incentives policies being introduced to encourage SLM practices by farmers and communities.

For example, in a study of smallholder farmers using participatory methods in Malawi, Cromwell et al. (2001) identified the following five factors used by farmers in Malawi as the most important indicators of sustainable agriculture:

- Crop diversification—growing a range of staple crops
- Access to adequate quantities of good seed—enough seed for timely planting at recommended spacing for all crops
- Farmland size—enough land to feed one's family
- Owning all the necessary farm tools and implements
- An optimal mix of crops for in-field soil fertility management through intercropping and relay planting (with legumes)

Not surprisingly, farmer concerns regarding sustainability of farming and cropping systems differ quite significantly, not only in spatial and temporal scales but also in scope, from the articulated priorities of researchers and policy makers (see Crosson and Anderson 1993).

CHAPTER FOUR

SLM Interventions: An Agri-technical Perspective

To stem the forbidding complexity of population pressure on an essentially fixed endowment of arable land, SLM and its associated curtailment of land degradation will require sustainable improvements in agricultural productivity. This necessarily entails not only the development of more input-responsive production technologies, but also a reduction of the real costs and the risks associated with input and output marketing.[7]

While input and output marketing should be ensured largely by the private sector, some government involvement is needed to facilitate efficient and transparent markets. The role of government will vary from country to country and by stage in the agricultural transformation process. The extent of the role will depend on factors such as the willingness of international agribusinesses and the capacity of the indigenous private sector to invest in input markets (which have high capital requirements and low profit margins), as well as farmers' effective demand for purchased inputs. This demand is dependent on the availability of profitable technology, on farm incomes and risk-bearing capabilities, and on farmers' knowledge of that technology and the financial capacity to invest in it.

As technologies requiring external input use are extended to more marginal production environments and poorer farmers, cost-effective ways to diminish or hedge and insure against downside risk will become critical to SLM. Important points to consider include:

- The possibility that inputs available for purchase may not be appropriate for all farmers.

- Whether alternative soil productivity–enhancing technologies, such as green manuring, minimum tillage, and improved fallows, may be financially and economically viable in riskier environments.
- The fact that complementary institutions and organizations are necessary to spread risk more evenly among farmers and input suppliers, thereby encouraging reliable use and repayment of bank or suppliers' credit.

An important corollary question is this: How can such institutions and organizations be designed and operated in a cost-effective way? In a review of successful land and resource management in African drylands, Reij and Steeds (2003) rated as success stories the remarkable resilience and adaptability of the people who inhabit drylands and the positive role of innovators. They identified the following contributing factors:

- Public support for private investment in soil and water conservation
- Systematic improvement of trunk roads
- Sound macroeconomic management, not discriminating against agriculture and natural resources
- Robust local capacity building by nongovernmental organizations, and other cooperative-type projects
- Consistent efforts by concerned governments since the mid-1980s to increase awareness of environmental problems and possible solutions

The Soil Fertility Initiative (SFI) was launched in 1996 in response to concerns of African stakeholders about land and natural resource degradation that were resulting in rapid declines in agricultural productivity. The SFI was co-sponsored by the World Bank, FAO, the CGIAR (represented by ICRAF), the International Fertilizer Development Corporation (IFDC), and several NGOs. The original goal of SFI was the introduction and adoption of sustainable soil fertility management practices by African smallholder farmers.

Although 20 Sub-Saharan countries endorsed SFI and several developed National Action Plans (NAP), very little national and international funding was made available for adequate and systematic implementation of SFI. The impact on the soil fertility management problem has been negligible (FAO 2002).

According to FAO (1999) the major constraints on the implementation of SFI Action Plans include:

- There has been a failure to recognize and address issues of national and regional ownership.
- There has been a lack of "champions" to motivate local, regional, and international stakeholders.
- Resources for coordination and facilitation and to operationalize the NAPs have been lacking.
- The SFI coalition expected the World Bank to provide coordination and facilitation, but this was not achieved.

- High turnover of local coordination staff led to a breakdown of the SFI coalition, a significant lack of operational funding, and significant delays in NAP preparation and implementation.
- Soil fertility problems are generally not recognized as critical issues in the PRSPs and CASs and hence do not receive resources via Bank lending operations—the notable exceptions are Burkina Faso and Guinea.

As a result of the dialogue generated by the early attempts to operationalize SFI, there is a regional consensus that lowland and farm productivity in Sub-Saharan Africa requires more than just mineral fertilizers and improved seed. The SFI concept has evolved to include integrated land and water management involving complementary organic and mineral sources of nutrients, crop and livestock diversification, and active links between indigenous knowledge and adaptive scientific research, backed by agricultural knowledge dissemination that involves farmer participation and experiential learning.

Targeted input programs for phosphorus fertilizer, seeds of appropriate legume crops, cover crops, and trees, coupled with payments for ecosystem and environmental services, will be necessary to jump start the SFI at local levels. International donor funding will be necessary to establish and sustain a coordination and facilitation unit to support NAP implementation.

The African Integrated Land and Water Management Initiative (ALWI), also sponsored by the Bank, was launched in 2001 to "contribute towards reversing the present trends of rapid natural resource degradation" with a strong focus on coordination among stakeholders to find synergies and reduce duplication of efforts related to improved resource management at catchment and watershed scales. In 2005, the World Bank supported the launch of TerrAfrica, a coalition of countries and stakeholders from Sub-Saharan Africa seeking to build on the lessons of SFI and ALWI and enhance SLM support.

As reflected above, SLM requires undertaking a complex and often interlocking set of actions to protect the existing land resource and curtail land degradation (box 4.1). These laudable objectives cannot be pursued (nor should they be) absent participation by farmers, other local residents, and other concerned stakeholders. To improve the prospects of success, it is the contention of this report that the authorities must find ways to align private interests (for example, the drive by rural households to secure basic needs, maintain income and consumption levels, enjoy some degree of food security, and mitigate risk) with the public's larger interest in SLM. But positive and negative incentives must be employed, and in locales where policy-induced disincentives and regulations might prove difficult to enforce, to every possible extent the emphasis will have to be placed on the application of positive incentives—for example, those that will contribute to improved real incomes and economic security while guaranteeing access to basic, often resource-based, needs.

Our vision is for land and natural resource managers (especially farmers) to become increasingly sensitive to consumer concerns about food quality and safety and the impact of agriculture on the environment. Most rural communities and land users would then be actively involved in various strategies to achieve sustainable, land management via:

- Increased planning and implementation of land and water management at the watershed scale
- Widespread awareness of the importance of both productive and environmental services of land and natural resource management
- Better targeting of farm inputs via precision farming and increased use of conservation and no-till and direct seeding farming methods
- Increased use of integrated crop protection methods and a significant reduction in pesticide use
- Integrated land and water management and optimization of farm nutrient balances through nutrient bookkeeping
- Major investments for manure storage and management in intensive livestock operations
- Protection of riparian zones via vegetative filter strips, rehabilitated wetlands, and zero tolerance for nutrient leakages into local streams
- More efficient water use in irrigation and the recycling of waste water

Source: Authors.

PROTECTING THE LAND RESOURCE: AGRICULTURAL INTENSIFICATION AND INTEGRATED FARMING SYSTEMS

Production practices that emphasize integrated land, plant nutrient, and water management are essential to SLM. The maintenance of native biodiversity can also be an important contributing factor. Biological diversity is required in a structural as well as a functional sense. Native stocks of available plant nutrients need to be managed to avoid having consumption exceed availability and, where necessary, ought to be supplemented from external (organic or chemical) sources in order to sustain system function and productivity.

The strategy of reducing risk by planting several species and crop varieties can stabilize yields over the long term, provide a range of dietary nutrients, and maximize returns with low levels of technology and limited resources. In drought-prone areas using low-input regimes with little supplemental water, these characteristics maximize labor efficiency per unit area of land, minimize the risk of catastrophic crop failure due to drought or severe pest attack, and guarantee the availability of food at medium to high levels of species productivity. There is a three-way interaction among biodiversity, ecosystem processes, and landscape dynamics. SLM practices that favor biodiversity maintenance at a regional level are also likely to benefit ecosystem services such as nutrient, water, and soil conservation; biological pest control; and efficient nutrient cycling.

Quite often, land degradation is accompanied by the proliferation of invasive and exotic weeds (for example, *Imperata cylindrica, Lantana camara, Chromolaena odorata,* and *Rubus moluccanus*). In Brazil, for example, the introduction of aggressive C4 pasture grasses (*Brachiaria humidicola* and *B. brizantha*) in the forest and *cerrado* regions means that natural regeneration of less aggressive native C3 species cannot occur very easily. The invasive weeds thus act to depress or eliminate native species. The control of invasive species is an essential component of the rehabilitation of degraded lands (Fernandes et al. 2006).

In South Africa, a mega-scale water conservation project, the Working for Water program, has been initiated with the dual aim of saving 10 percent of the annual runoff and protecting native biodiversity by means of a countrywide clearing of invasive alien water-consuming plants. The effort will engage some 40,000 individuals over a 30-year period. The goal is to improve rain-fed agriculture by reducing the hydroclimatic constraints to rain-fed crop production and by making supplementary irrigation an efficient means to increase otherwise poor crop yields. This is an example of how SLM practices can be used to manage the partitioning of rainwater between the vertical green and the horizontal blue water pools via clearing, reforestation, afforestation, and cropping system management.

SOIL FERTILITY MANAGEMENT

An important component of SLM is the management of soil and plant nutrients. Soil fertility can be improved by managing nutrient stocks and flows (where inputs exceed or balance outputs). A range of intervention strategies are available to farmers (Scoones and Toulmin 1999):

- Nutrient recapitalization—for example, adding phosphorus via a one-time application of rock phosphate
- Applying inorganic fertilizers together with lime to control soil acidity
- Using organic manures and legumes to fix atmospheric nitrogen
- Combining organic and inorganic nutrient sources

Plant nutrients are usually removed from the crop and forest systems via harvests of grain, tubers, fruit, and wood and also by surface erosion and subsurface leaching. Land users tend to purchase and use fertilizer nutrients in areas with good market access and higher agricultural potential. In order for farmers to realize the yield potential due to added fertilizers, it is essential that they have access to good (improved) seed. Major constraints to farmers purchasing fertilizers include one or more of the following: (a) high cost of fertilizer, (b) lack of cash or credit to purchase the fertilizer, and (c) low prices for the increased yields from added fertilizer.

In agroecologically less favored areas, farmers can use a variety of risk-minimization strategies based on biological sources of nutrients, adapted crop varieties or species, and integrated land and water management. The literature on integrated nutrient management documents the following generic practices for effective nutrient management and sustainable cropping:

- *Minimize soil erosion and leaching.* The most effective way to reduce soil erosion and leaching is to maximize soil cover via the use of cover crops and mulches and by integrating perennials in vegetative strips along the contours to further stabilize the soil. Where soil depth is adequate, such vegetative strips permit interstrip erosion and result in a gradual leveling of the slope and in terrace formation without the need for labor intensive manual terrace formation. Soil's organic matter (humus) is essential for maintaining its physical and chemical environment for plant growth as well as hydrologic functions. In semiarid rain-fed systems, inputs of crop residues and other forms of plant biomass are often insufficient (or have other priority uses) to maintain critical levels of organic matter. Under these conditions, conservation or minimum tillage significantly reduces soil carbon oxidation following the planting of each crop (and also frees up labor for other activities). Conservation and no-till farming can also significantly reduce soil erosion (Pieri et al. 2002). Note that some erosion is desirable for maintaining downstream and coastal habitats and ecosystem processes.
- *Recycle organic nutrients.* One method is to return all crop residues to the field of origin. In many cases, however, crop residues are fed to livestock. Ideally the livestock should be fed the residues in the field so that the manure goes directly onto the soil. If the residues are removed and fed to livestock elsewhere, the manure should be returned to the field as soon as possible. The transport and spreading of manure on fields, however, is often a problem because of labor constraints. The composting of vegetable residues and the use of animal manure is an efficient way to conserve farm nutrients and enable farmers to redistribute the nutrient-rich compost to fields during periods when demand for scarce labor is low. Combining manures with inorganic fertilizers can result in significant synergy and increased nutrient and water use efficiencies (Piha 1993). One desirable goal is the ability to manipulate SOM dynamics via management practices to promote soil conservation, to ensure the sustainable productivity of agroecosystems, and to increase the capacity of tropical soils to act as a sink for, rather than a source of, atmospheric carbon (Fernandes et al. 1997).
- *Enhance biological sources of nutrients.* Nitrogen-fixing trees, shrubs, and herbaceous and crop species can fix nitrogen from the atmosphere and

make it available to subsequent crops via biological or associative nitrogen fixation.

- *Compensate for nutrient loss.* Add nutrients first as green or animal manure and, if necessary, top off with inorganic fertilizers. Where soil nutrients have been severely depleted, it is often necessary to restore the minimum levels required for adequate plant growth and yield. Sanchez et al. (1997) have argued for nutrient recapitalization (especially of phosphorus) in Sub-Saharan Africa as a means of priming the biological nitrogen-fixation process and improving crop productivity. Animal manure and plant litters are generally low in phosphorus, and phosphorus, unlike nitrogen, cannot be fixed from the atmosphere. Phosphorus deficiency is a major constraint on effective nitrogen fixation because phosphorus is an important nutrient in the process of nodulation and nitrogen fixation. Guano (for both nitrogen and phosphorus) and rock phosphate (phosphorus and calcium) can be good sources of phosphorus where such materials are available locally (for example, in Peru, Madagascar, Zaire, and West Africa).

- *Select and use adapted and efficient species.* Some leguminous tree and crop species are able to fix nitrogen at very low levels of available soil phosphorus. Leguminous crops that combine some grain yield with high levels of root and leaf biomass, and thus a low nitrogen harvest, offer a useful compromise in meeting farmers' food security concerns and improving soil fertility. On-farm nitrogen budgets indicate that the use of legumes with high-quality residues and deep root systems is an effective way of improving nutrient cycling.

- *Optimize fertilizer-rainfall interactions.* Rainfall markedly affects fertilizer use efficiency, yet there is almost no guidacne as how farmers should adjust fertilizer use to seasonal rainfall. Piha (1993) developed and modified "response farming" techniques that use early rainfall events to decide on the amounts of fertilizer to apply in any given season. Over a five-year period, Piha's system gave 25–42% more yield and 21–41% more profit than did the existing fertilizer recommendations. The key to the system was its flexibility. In poor years, fertilizer nitrogen use was reduced, but yields would be poor in those years in any case. In good years, the farmer could get good yields. Participating farmers' profits were 105% higher than those of the control group of comparably good farmers. Yields were 78% higher. Loan repayment was excellent at 90%. Yet Piha's work has yet to be recognized a decade later.

MARKET OPPORTUNITIES LINKED TO EROSION CONTROL PRACTICES: A KEY TO ADOPTION?

In the developing countries of the tropics, hillside agriculture is often characterized by a vicious circle of poverty reinforcing environmental degradation. Most of the poor people employed in farming reside in the fragile ecosystems of the mid-altitude hillsides. Mining the natural resource base gives farmers short-term subsistence, but creates a profound discrepancy between actual systems of land use and the ecologically sound systems appropriate for fragile soils on steep slopes. Maintenance of the natural resource base on the hillsides is thus of vital importance not only to ensure the future livelihood of resource-poor farmers, but also to restrain rural-urban drift, at least until urban centers are better positioned to accept increased numbers of rural migrants.

Soil erosion has been identified as one of the most pressing resource management problems on the hillsides. In Central America alone, for example, over 60 percent of the hillsides are subject to severe water erosion caused by agriculture. Although an abundance of erosion control technologies exists, adoption of these technologies in tropical countries has been disappointing. In many cases, soil depletion is rational from the farmer's point of view (Ashby 1985; Anderson and Thampapillai 1990). As the soil degenerates, however, yield and income losses build up. At early stages of soil depletion, the net returns without soil conservation exceed the net returns with conservation. Over time, as soil degenerates further, the gap declines, until eventually net returns with conservation are higher than those without. Adoption of soil conservation technologies is unlikely to occur before this point, which one study calculates to be at least 40 to 60 years after degeneration begins, depending on the discount rate used (Seitz et al. 1979), and this can lead to a conflict between the farmer's logic and ecological considerations.

Studies also suggest that even when farmers are aware of the monetary benefits of erosion control, such as yield increases, they are unlikely to be concerned with nonmonetary benefits, such as soil resilience, or with downstream benefits that accrue to others. Thus, the extent to which soil conservation practices are voluntarily adopted by farmers will often prove suboptimal from society's point of view.

The problems with adoption of the soil conservation practices discussed above imply that farmers will have to be offered incentives to induce timely adoption. Incentives have commonly taken the form of subsidies or regulations. The former are costly, and in many cases induce distortions in other sectors of the economy. The latter are extremely difficult to enforce. The research reported here explores a different type of incentive. The objective is to link income earning and/or cost-saving opportunities to soil conservation practices (box 4.2). This is expected to increase the returns to conservation practices, resulting in earlier adoption of sustainable practices.

In many cases, adoption of soil conservation practices may in fact occur because of the opportunity to increase income, with soil conservation occurring as a by-product. This approach derives support from the fact that, in the few cases of successful adoption that have occurred, soil conservation practices permitted the introduction of high-value crops, supported the introduction of livestock, or generated income by being associated with value-added processes (Nimlos and Savage 1991; Tiffen and Mortimore 1992). Linking

Two well-known examples of payments by lowland communities for ecosystems services provided by upland communities can be found in New York City and in the Cauca Valley of Colombia. In 1989, New York's water, piped in from the Catskill Mountains, was found to contain rising levels of sediments and pollutants. The Environmental Protection Agency ordered the city to build a water filtration plant at an estimated cost of between US$ 6 billion and 8 billion. Instead of building the expensive filtration plant, however, the city opted to work with the residents of the Catskills watershed. They financed reforestation projects, created riparian woodlands to protect the integrity of the streams, and signed conservation easements with local farmers to enhance the filtration of sediments and pollutants by the riparian vegetation. The quality of the water improved dramatically, and the cost of this collaborative effort with the residents of the Catskills was less than US$ 2 billion—a big saving to New York City taxpayers. Similarly, in Colombia's Cauca Valley, agricultural producers pay fees, via their water-user associations, to compensate upland communities for soil conservation on steep slopes, reforestation, and maintenance of riparian vegetation buffers to improve water flows and reduce sedimentation in irrigation canals.

Source: Pagiola et al. 2002.

market opportunity to conservation practices is vital, however. The literature is replete with cases in which the introduction of income-generating opportunities without any links to conservation have exacerbated resource degradation (Thrupp 1993).

In particular, upland farmers lack information about marketing opportunities. This information could widen the range of crops grown to include those that can positively contribute to curtailing soil erosion. There is evidence from the Bank's Europe and Central Asia region that vertical marketing systems that link farmer producers to product processors might facilitate the exploitation of new market opportunities by small-scale farmers.

PROTECTING AND MANAGING WATERSHEDS

Investments in watershed management are critical to the sustainability of land and water resources (see figure 4.1). In upland areas, set-asides, reforestation, and soil conservation on a large scale are essential. In floodplains, land zoning to provide space for inevitable flooding is preferable to enormously costly (and

Figure 4.1 Effects of Land and Water Management at the Watershed Level

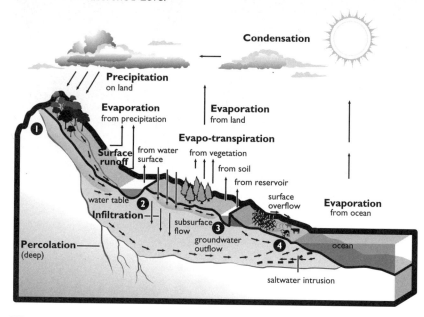

Water evaporates from rivers, lakes, and soil. Plants transpire water during photosynthesis and respiration (transpiration). Direct evaporation from the soil and transpiration from plants is collectively termed evapotranspiration. Transpiration rates vary according to vegetation type due to differences in leaf area and the depth and density of root systems. Consequently, changes in vegetation type in response to land management practices can have significant impacts on the water balance at subcatchment and catchment scales. The total volume of evapotranspiration from a vegetated land surface depends on vegetation type, climate, and soil factors. In the figure above, the forests at the top of the catchment (1) are important for both interception of rainfall and partitioning the rainfall into surface and subsurface flows. Reservoirs and small dams (2 + 3) serve to collect and hold surface flow for local use but also create additional surfaces for evaporation of water that may have infiltrated into the soil. Plantations of fast-growing species can increase evapotranspiration and reduce subsurface flows. Intensive land use in riparian (river bank) areas can increase sediment and nutrient (especially nitrogen) loads to water bodies.

Source: Adapted from Keenan et al. 2004.

often eventually unsuccessful) efforts to control floods (Grey and Sadoff 2002). Table 4.1 presents an organizing framework for SLM-related interventions that have been shown to enhance watershed functions and productivity.

The following "best practices" can be envisaged for assessment of the costs and benefits of successful watershed management for equitable upstream-downstream resources management:

Table 4.1	Organizing Framework for Technical Aspects of Land and Natural Resource Management at the Watershed Level	
Watershed objectives	**Land use management**	**Structural approaches and methods**
Sustain or increase land productivity.	■ Intensify land management, replenish soil nutrients, and control soil acidity by liming and organic inputs. ■ Select and use adapted crop, forage, and tree species. ■ Manage grazing and eliminate the use of fires for land clearing and pasture reclamation. ■ Maintain soil cover via cover crops and residue recycling. ■ Protect and stabilize slopes. ■ Use water harvesting and efficient irrigation where possible. ■ Maintain drainage to prevent waterlogging and salinity build-up.	■ Contour plantings, vegetative strips, and terraces ■ Grading and reservoirs to facilitate water harvesting and subsequent redistribution ■ Irrigation and drainage canals (installation and maintenance)
Provide adequate quantity of water.	■ Use soil cover to enhance water infiltration and prevent soil crusting. ■ Use crop, forage, and tree species with high water-use efficiencies.	■ Water-harvesting structures ■ Irrigation, reservoirs, and well facilities ■ Desalinization where no cheaper freshwater supplies are available
Maintain water quality.	■ Protect vegetative filter areas in riparian zones and wetlands to remove excess sediment and nutrients (nitrogen, phosphorus). ■ Manage household and livestock waste to prevent pollution of surface and ground water.	■ Water treatment facilities ■ Alternative supplies
Reduce flooding and flood damage.	■ Protect and maintain wetlands and zone and regulate floodplains. ■ Plant deep-rooted vegetation to enhance infiltration and water consumption by plants.	■ Water diversion structures and reservoir flood control ■ Levees and gully control structures ■ Installing and maintaining drainage channels

Source: Adapted from FAO 1995.

- All parties in the watershed have a stake in the management program and watershed development functions as an equity-enhancing mechanism.
- Because irrigation water is often the most valuable resource of watershed management, it is essential to develop mechanisms that allow an equitable sharing of the water. This *resource sharing* can substitute for direct payments to some stakeholders.
- Where common property is involved, especially in the upper catchments, it is essential that local communities collectively protect the common land so that the irrigation water resource is not compromised by illegal deforestation or overgrazing. Collective action is easier where communities are homogeneous.
- The benefits of good resource management and water harvesting for irrigation in watersheds will vary with agroclimatic and biophysical conditions. If the benefits are not sufficiently substantial to be meaningfully shared, environmental service payments may not be economically viable.
- Leverage for the landless and less powerful stakeholders in the watershed is necessary to enable them to participate effectively in the program. In some cases, external institutions may need to play a facilitating role on behalf of the "weakest" stakeholders.
- If irrigation water is used to produce greater vegetation biomass on common lands, biomass-sharing agreements are needed, especially for landless stakeholders.
- If water harvesting results in improved recharge of groundwater aquifers, designating ground water as a common property resource can provide all stakeholders with a powerful incentive to improve natural resource management practices and collective action.

EXPLOITING THE PRODUCTION AND ENVIRONMENTAL SERVICE FUNCTIONS OF LAND

In addition to facilitating the production of food, feeds, and industrial crops, natural ecosystems and agroecosystems also provide a wide variety of "non-market" services. The environmental services derived from forest ecosystems typically include (but are not limited to):

- Hydrological benefits: controlling the timing and volume of water flows and protecting water quality
- Reduced sedimentation: avoiding damage to downstream reservoirs and waterways, thereby safeguarding uses such as hydroelectric power generation, irrigation, recreation, fisheries, and domestic water supplies
- Disaster mitigation: buffering against floods and landslides
- Biodiversity conservation
- Carbon sequestration and sinks for other greenhouse gases such as methane

- Do forests increase runoff? Because of increased interception, transpiration, and deeper rooting depth in forests than in crop- or grasslands, catchment studies show that annual runoff is generally decreased under forests.
- Do forests regulate flows? Increased dry-season transpiration but increased infiltration and, for cloud forests, cloud-water deposition, may augment dry-season flows. More and more evidence from catchments worldwide shows that most forests reduce dry-season flows. Infiltration properties are critical in partitioning runoff. The effects are site specific, so more research is needed.
- Do forests reduce erosion? Natural forestland is associated with high infiltration rates and low soil erosion, but plantations may not show these benefits because of roads, ditches, and splash erosion. Forest canopies may not protect soil from the impact of raindrops. More research is needed on species and drop size.

Source: Calder 2005.

Although forested ecosystems are often perceived as providing many beneficial services, it does not always follow that reforestation of landscapes automatically results in benefits to downstream ecosystems and users (Calder 2005). Empirical evidence from a number of watershed studies shows that substituting grass and herbaceous vegetation with trees can result in significantly different and, in semiarid and subhumid areas, often negative consequences for dry-season water flows (box 4.3). This is an important finding given the considerable investments in reforestation and afforestation projects globally.

The Forestry Research Program of the UK Department for International Development (DFID) has produced a very insightful synthesis of the impact of deforestation and reafforestation on water flows. The synthesis was based on empirical work conducted in well-designed projects using improved instrumentation, better mathematical modeling, and powerful geographic information systems to produce more reliable prediction of the association between vegetation (including forests) and streamflows. The findings of the integrated research approach are summarized in ten lessons for policy makers and natural resource management project managers (FRP 2005):

1. If water shortages are a problem in dry countries, impose limits on forest plantations, especially of fast-growing evergreen species.

2. Implement "green water" instruments (based on data from plant transpiration) to control levels of evaporation from upland vegetation.
3. If upland forests are cleared for cultivation, provide farmers with guidelines for best agricultural practices.
4. Any market mechanism or tax system linking land management to quantified streamflow should ensure that scientific validation is possible at the scale of the operation.
5. Use decision support systems to assess the impact of alternative land management options on water resources, and of alternative land use and water management and policy options on different social groups.
6. Ensure that policy instruments are equitable in terms of livelihood benefits, not just water allocation.
7. Ensure that any proposed market mechanism is adequately pro-poor.
8. Consider improvements in rain-fed farming (crop breeding, rainwater harvesting, mulching, conservation tillage, market access, capacity building) in preference to further investments in rural small-scale irrigation schemes.
9. Use negotiation support system techniques such as choice experiments to ascertain stakeholder preferences for policy agreements.
10. Tailor employment programs to dovetail with other livelihood activities of the people whom they are intended to attract.

Payments for environmental services (PES) could significantly improve and diversify the income sources of land users, especially in the developing world. There are a variety of existing market-based mechanisms and criteria for rewarding good natural resources management via payments for the resulting environmental services. For trading purposes, the services need to be tangible, scientifically quantified, and in accordance with local legislation (Pagiola et al. 2002). The payment mechanisms include private deals, public payments, and open trading schemes among local communities, municipalities, companies, and national governments. Economic valuation offers a way to compare the diverse benefits and costs associated with ecosystems by attempting to measure them and expressing them in a common denominator—typically a monetary unit used (see table 4.2). The main framework used is the Total Economic Value approach (Pearce and Warford 1993).

The market-based incentive systems that provide rewards in the hope of promoting sustainable land and water stewardship in catchments and basins generally work on the concept that enhanced resources management in upper catchments results in both productivity and ecosystem services that can benefit stakeholders in the lower catchments. In most incentive-based systems, the beneficiaries are charged an appropriate amount that is then equitably shared among the land users in the upper catchment.

Emerging markets for payments for ecosystem services in Costa Rica (Miranda et al. 2003), India, the United States, and Australia have resulted in some positive behavioral changes in resource management on the part of upstream land users—with significant downstream benefits (Pagiola et al. 2002). Watershed services are very dependent on the watershed or subwatershed level, however, which limits market scale and size.

To ensure the success and sustainability of incentive-based systems to facilitate the improved management of irrigation water and associated natural resources, the following challenges may have to be overcome:

- Identifying and reliably quantifying the volume and quality of water flows and associated benefits (for example, vegetation biomass and soil cover, reduced erosion, and added food and fiber production) provided by good land and natural resources stewardship.
- Identifying the risks (for example, climate change) and opportunities for mitigating the risk to irrigation water and natural resources management operations (Burton and van Aalst 2004).
- Identifying the beneficiaries of the improved volume and quality of water flows and charging them to provide the financing mechanism.
- Ensuring that payments are equitably distributed to all stakeholders and that the amount not only compensates them for the costs of changes in resources management but also reflects the value of the services provided. Because supply price and ecosystem benefits are based on location in the watershed or landscape, Chomitz et al. (1998) suggest a framework based on spatial information to guide prioritization and pricing.
- Creating an appropriate decision-making framework and institutional support structure that can be accessed by all stakeholders. Watershed-modeling tools are also very useful in engaging community, research, and policy stakeholders (Calder 2005).

Although biodiversity itself is not an ecosystem service, conserving biodiversity can promote a wide range of ecosystem benefits and environmental services. It is the ecological interaction of taxonomic and functional groups of biota that maintain ecosystem function and provide a measure of resilience in the face of environmental shocks. Loss of biodiversity is commonly associated with a loss of system function that, in extreme cases, can lead to irreversible system breakdown. Rural farmers in marginally productive lands tend to be more acutely aware of the relationship between biodiversity and its role in the maintenance of livelihoods than are their counterparts, broad-scale agriculturalists. The irony for the rural poor is that a downward economic spiral rarely provides any leeway for biodiversity conservation. Under such circumstances, providing incentives directly through monetary payments, or indirectly through policy instruments that facilitate some form of tax relief, is most likely to generate positive feedback for land management and sustainable livelihoods (box 4.4).

Although there are, as yet, no efficient mechanisms for the economic calibration of naturally occurring and farm-based biodiversity, recent studies in

Table 4.2 Economic Valuation Techniques for PES

Methodology	Approach	Applications	Data requirements	Limitations
Revealed preference methods				
Production function (also known as "change in productivity")	Trace effect of change in ecosystem services on produced goods.	Anything that affects produced goods	Change in service, effect on production, net value of produced goods	Data on change in service and consequent impact on production are often lacking.
Cost of illness, human capital	Trace effect of change in ecosystem services on morbidity and mortality.	Anything that affects health (e.g., air or water pollution)	Change in service, effect on health (dose-response functions), cost of illness or value of life	Dose-response functions linking environmental conditions to health are often lacking; under-estimates result because preferences for health are omitted; value of life cannot easily be estimated.
Replacement cost (and variants, such as relocation cost)	Use cost of replacing the lost good or service.	Any loss of goods or services	Extent of loss of goods or services, cost of replacing them	Tends to overestimate actual value; should be used with caution.
Travel cost (TCM)	Derive demand curve from data on actual travel costs.	Recreation	Survey to collect data on monetary and time costs of travel to destination, distance traveled	Limited to recreational benefits; hard to use when trips are to multiple destinations.

Hedonic pricing	Extract effect of environmental factors on price of goods that include those factors.	Air quality, scenic beauty, cultural benefits	Prices and characteristics of goods	Requires vast quantities of data; very sensitive to specification.
Stated preference methods				
Contingent valuation (CV)	Ask respondents directly their WTP for a specified service.	Any service	Survey that presents a scenario and elicits WTP for specified service	Many potential sources of bias in responses; guidelines exist for reliable application.
Choice modeling	Ask respondents to choose their preferred option from a set of alternatives with particular attributes.	Any service	Survey of respondents	Similar to CV; analysis of the data generated is complex.
Other methods				
Benefits transfer	Use results obtained in one context in a different context.	Any for which suitable comparison studies are available	Valuation exercises at a similar site	Can be very inaccurate, as many factors vary even when contexts seem "similar"; should be used with caution.

Source: Pagiola et al. 2004.
Note: WTP—Willingness to pay for a benefit or service.

Low food crop productivity and a growing population have led to substantial clearing of forestland for agricultural use in Madagascar, threatening the country's unique biodiversity. A protected-areas system was created in an effort to conserve biodiversity. Protection of these areas has succeeded in substantially slowing deforestation within their boundaries. However, with an estimated 70 percent of the population living below the poverty line in 2001, many have asked whether it makes sense to spend resources on protected areas and prevent the use of their land and timber resources.

The figure below illustrates the results of a study undertaken to estimate the costs and benefits of the protected-areas system in terms of their present value over a 10-year period. The first column shows the total flow of benefits from the protected-areas system. Despite the high management costs and the forgone income from use of that land, the system is estimated to provide net benefits to the country thanks to the valuable watershed protection services these areas provide, their tourism benefits, and the payments received for biodiversity conservation. But, as the breakdown on the right side of the figure shows, these benefits are very unevenly distributed. Local communities bear the brunt of the costs, because they are barred from using the protected areas either for agriculture or for the collection of fuelwood and other nontimber forest products (NTFPs). Downstream water users, such as farmers who use irrigation, benefit substantially, as do tourism operators.

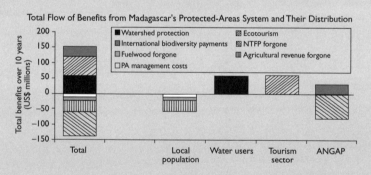

Total Flow of Benefits from Madagascar's Protected-Areas System and Their Distribution

Source: Carret and Loyer 2003.

These results confirmed that, although international biodiversity payments and ecotourism revenues make protected areas beneficial for Madagascar, appropriate, compensation mechanisms are needed for local communities if these protected areas are to be sustained.

Source: Adapted from Pagiola et al. 2004.

Southeast Asia and Latin America (Gillison 2000, 2002) have shown how relatively low-cost baseline surveys can provide a model for coupling biodiversity with potential agricultural productivity and profitability (total factor profitability), including above-ground carbon. Models of this kind show promise in identifying and calibrating indicators that can be used to attach an economic value to biodiversity. To put such methods into practice will require a system of user-friendly field indicators derived from representative regional baseline studies. Among the relatively simple indicators that have been established so far is a relative measure of vegetation or plant diversity known as the "V" index (see appendix). The emergence of this and other simple science-based indicators is providing a generic, rapid, low-cost approach to valuing biodiversity. Further critical testing is envisioned in contrasting ecological zones before such indicators can be implemented with confidence.

The Bank's Evolving SLM Portfolio

C urrently the World Bank's country operational frameworks, such as poverty reduction strategy papers, country assistance strategies (CAS), strategic environmental assessments, country environmental analyses, and so on, affect the preparation of SLM and other forms of natural resource projects. Each has aimed to address many of the issues directly or indirectly involved in integrating land and water management, biodiversity conservation, and the environment.

PAST AND CURRENT INVESTMENTS FOR SLM AND RELATED INTERVENTIONS

The Bank's rural development strategy *Reaching the Rural Poor* (World Bank 2003) specifically targets the "enhanced sustainability of natural resource management." To promote the conservation and restoration of natural assets in rural areas, the Bank has developed guidelines and strategies for the environment, forestry, and water, and explicitly links rural development in agriculture to sustainable, resource management. In addition, the in-country poverty-reduction strategy program (PRSP) approach has been supported with a Poverty-Reduction Strategy Source Book available on the World Bank's web site that has sections on natural resources and related concerns.

THE PATTERN OF BANK GROUP INVESTMENTS IN SLM, NRM, BIOCARBON, AND WATERSHED MANAGEMENT PROGRAMS

The World Bank, the International Finance Corporation, the Global Environment Facility, and other donors have supported SLM projects through the provision of significant loans and grants over several decades.[8] The investments include:

- International Bank for Reconstruction and Development (IBRD) and International Development Assistance (IDA) projects with SLM as a component (1999–2004)
- IBRD and IDA projects focusing on watershed management
- World Bank carbon investment funds (2002–2005)

IBRD and IDA Projects with SLM as a Component (1999–2004)

Since 1990, there have been investments in approximately 250 projects with SLM components within agriculture, forestry, natural resource management, land rehabilitation, mining, and land administration across the Bank's six regions. The projects dealt with SLM field activities or the organizational, policy, and technical means to implement SLM and to create the enabling conditions necessary to induce land management change (for example, the provision of secure land title). Target groups or implementing participants were either the government or multiple partners that included government, industry, community groups, and individual land users. See table 5.1 for a detailed list of SLM practices targeted in IBRD and IDA investments.

A review of implementation completion reports for 47 projects in which the SLM component comprised more than 25 percent of the total investment revealed that between 1990 and 2000, 34 projects (72 percent) involved substantially sustainable natural resource management components. Of the total lending of $2.6 billion allocated to the 47 projects, $2.0 billion went to the sustainable NRM-oriented projects. This constituted 74 percent of the total lending allocated to the 47 projects (figure 5.1). The range of SLM investments across sectors is presented in table 5.1.

The SLM projects had a high rate of success in achieving the intended project outcomes. The economic rate of return (ERR) estimated for all project expenditures ranged between 6.7 and 34 percent, averaging 21.8 percent. Although this is a relatively small sample, the figures are indicative of the high variability in performance among the projects. The agriculture sector and the land rehabilitation projects that were agriculturally oriented provided significant gains in improving rural livelihoods. The coupling of SLM activities with

Table 5.1 Summary of SLM Strategies Implemented across Sectors

Approach \ Sector	Irrigation and drainage	Crops	Forestry	Agricultural research and extension	Flood protection	General agriculture	Natural resource management	Animal production	Environment	Other social services
Watershed management				X		X	X			
Terracing				X		X				
Irrigation or drainage system	X	X		X	X	X				
Soil fertility management	X	X		X						
Soil erosion management	X	X	X	X	X	X	X			
Moisture conservation	X	X		X		X				
Crop introduction		X		X	X					
Crop diversification		X		X		X				
Crop intensification	X			X		X				
Research capacity building		X		X			X	X		
Extension capacity building				X			X	X		
Technology transfer capacity building	X	X		X			X	X		
Technology generation capacity building		X	X	X			X	X		
Use of participatory approach			X	X			X			
Institutional capacity building	X		X		X		X	X		
Rural income generation	X	X	X	X	X	X	X	X		
Policy reform							X			
Supporting input and credit services	X	X		X		X	X	X		
Providing alternatives to slash and burn		X								
Poverty alleviation	X	X	X	X			X	X		
Biodiversity conservation		X		X	X		X	X		
Deforestation control		X		X			X	X		
Improved access to land	X			X		X	X			
Reducing overgrazing				X						
Microcatchment development	X			X			X			
Export crop enhancement	X			X						
Surveying land use	X									
Silviculture intensification			X				X			
Environmental monitoring										

Source: Authors.

Figure 5.1   Actual World Bank Lending by Region for Sustainable
Natural Resource Management Projects with More Than
25 Percent of Total for SLM

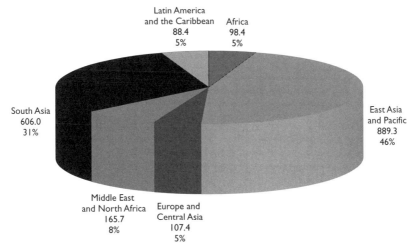

Latin America
and the Caribbean   Africa
88.4   98.4
5%   5%

South Asia
606.0
31%

East Asia
and Pacific
889.3
46%

Middle East
and North Africa   Europe and
165.7   Central Asia
8%   107.4
5%

Source: Authors.

improvements in land administration enabled private land users to improve their land management practices. Forestry projects achieved SLM primarily through the strengthening of government enterprises, with a high ERR estimated for many projects because of the provision of management for established forests that had often been neglected because of a scarcity of funds. The overall achievement of project objectives (outcomes) by the reviewed SLM projects was high, with 80 percent of projects (32) rated as "satisfactory" or better, and only eight projects rated as "unsatisfactory" or "highly unsatisfactory." Africa had the highest number of unsatisfactory projects.

Stakeholder participation emerged as a major factor contributing to the success of SLM-type projects. The main methods of achieving effective participation included:

- The involvement of all relevant stakeholders, no matter how remote they may be (for example, nomadic grazers), which ensures that the land uses and management activities of all system players are considered.
- The early involvement of stakeholders during the project design phase and throughout implementation to promote ownership and commitment at different levels (government, implementing agency, project implementation unit, land users, and communities).
- Providing adequate time for participatory planning and unambiguous land use rights.

- Participatory activities that facilitated experiential learning and the harnessing of local knowledge to readjust and refine programs and the development of innovative approaches.

IBRD and IDA Projects Focusing on Watershed Management

A selection of the major World Bank watershed management (WSM) regional projects and levels of investment from 1990 to 2004 is presented in table 5.2. Almost all the WSM projects had sustainable NRM and SLM as their top priority, followed by institutional capacity building and then agricultural productivity. Over half of the projects addressed land degradation with active stakeholder participation. Surprisingly, the project documents offer very few references to policy and legal framework support and to land tenure issues.

World Bank Carbon Investment Funds (2002–2005)

Market research by the World Bank showed that during 2002, worldwide trading of credits in greenhouse gas emissions tripled to an estimated 67 million tons of carbon dioxide equivalent as companies prepared for the ratification of the Kyoto Protocol. But the same study also showed that only 13 percent of direct private-sector carbon emission reduction purchases were made from projects in the developing world. High transaction costs and the uncertainties of dealing in new and unfamiliar markets deterred most potential investors. To help develop these markets, the World Bank launched the Community Development Carbon Fund in April 2003 to provide carbon finance to small-scale projects in the least developed countries. And in November 2003, the Bank announced the BioCarbon Fund. This is a public and private initiative to finance projects that sequester carbon in vegetation and soils ("carbon sinks") while helping to reverse land degradation, conserve biodiversity, and improve the livelihoods of local communities (Newcombe 2003).

The scope of the BioCarbon Fund covers the entire range of land use activities. The kinds of projects financed by the fund include:

- Small SLM-oriented reforestation projects to restore landscape stability by reducing erosion and providing windbreaks.
- Reforestation projects to conserve and protect unique and endangered forest ecosystems by connecting forest fragments with corridors to create viable long-term habitats.
- Agroforestry projects such as those to shade coffee, intercrop trees with other crops, and establish trees to help restore degraded grazing lands.
- Projects for community-promoted planting of timber, biofuel, and other forest products that fit within a broader landscape design.
- Projects for improved forest management to enhance carbon storage in the transition economies of Eastern Europe and the former Soviet Union. (World Bank 2006a).

Table 5.2 Selected Examples of Investments for Watershed Management Programs in Different Regions: World Bank Watershed Management Projects (1990–2004)

Country	Project type or name	Total project cost US$ million	Total World Bank Investment US$ million	WB % of total
Africa				
Burkina Faso	Environmental management project	25.5	16.5	65
Mali	Natural resources management project	32.1	20.4	64
East Asia and Pacific				
Indonesia	Yogyakarta Upland Area Development Project	25.1	15.5	62
China	Second Red Soils Area Development Project	296.4	150	51
China	Loess Plateau Watershed Rehabilitation Project	248.7	150	60
Eastern and Central Asia				
Turkey	Eastern Anatolia Watershed Rehabilitation Project	115.5	82.1	71
Turkey	Anatolia Watershed Rehabilitation Project	248.7	150	60
Latin America and the Caribbean				
Brazil	Land Management II Project–Santa Catarina	71.6	33	46
Brazil	Land Management III Project	124.7	55	44
Middle East and North Africa				
Tunisia	Northwest Mountainous Areas Development Project	50.7	27.5	54
Morocco	Lakhdar Watershed Management Pilot Project	5.8	4	69
South Asia Region				
India	Integrated Watershed Development (Plains) Project	91.8	62	68
India	Integrated Watershed Development (Hills) Project	125.6	88	70
India	Integrated Watershed Development (Hills-II) Project	193	135	70

Source: Darghouth and others (in preparation).

Figure 5.2 BioCarbon Projects by Region

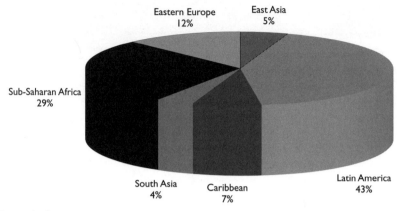

Source: Authors.

Latin America (US$ 25 million) and Africa (US$ 15 million) account for the major share of the carbon sequestration projects approved for certified emissions reduction (CER) credits (figure 5.2). The bulk of the investments currently target environmental plantings, agroforestry, and community reforestation programs (figure 5.3). There are currently major European objections to the inclusion of agricultural sinks for CER under the clean development mechanism projects covered in window 1 of the Kyoto Protocol. This is un-

Figure 5.3 Carbon Value of BioCarbon Projects by Land Management Category

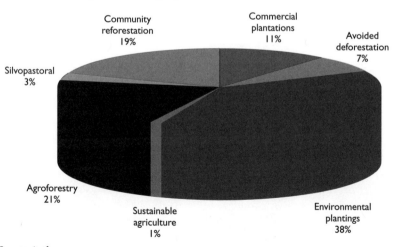

Source: Authors.

fortunate, because if agricultural sinks were eligible, the resulting increases in sequestered soil carbon (that is, more soil organic matter) would also have a significant beneficial effect on soil biological, chemical, and physical properties (Ingram and Fernandes 2001), which would result in greater nutrient and water-holding capacity and thus enhance productivity and promote further investments in SLM.

LESSONS LEARNED

Because land and natural resource management issues vary greatly from community to community, from watershed to watershed, and from country to country, it is simplistic to generalize about outcomes. We examined the World Bank's Operations Evaluation Department (World Bank 1988) review of investment experiences in NRM, where 12 country case studies were undertaken to examine the Bank's operations through economic and sector work (ESW) and project lending during the period 1965 to 1986.

The conceptual framework used by the OED to evaluate successful NRM was based on the following principles:

- Sustainability is likely when renewable resources are properly used and conserved rather than depleted.
- Economic efficiency is essential.
- The resulting benefits must be equitably distributed.

The OED review also assumed that, although in practice conflicts arise and choices have to be made, any use of renewable resources that leads to the exhaustion of those resources cannot be efficient. Furthermore, although trade-offs between equity and sustainability or equity and efficiency may exist in the short run, the concept of equity implies that over the long term, management must promote equity for future generations, too. The lessons described in the OED report are instructive and very valuable to current analyses of investment approaches and trends, so we summarize them here.

1. ESW products produced between 1965 and 1986 generally did not provide the strategic framework for specifically identifying the main natural resource (including land) management issues in a country and the options for dealing with them. The result, therefore, was an opportunistic approach whereby the selection and design of projects was influenced more by policy papers.
2. In all countries, resource management is governed by social and institutional arrangements that are as complex as they are sensitive. Often little is known about the interactions between the socioeconomic and natural systems. (These days, the Bank is very alert to safeguard issues—social and indigenous rights, environmental protection, development policy lending, and environmental impact assessments.)

3. The indications are that environmental issues frequently were inadequately addressed during project design. Such issues, therefore, often got little attention in the supervision reports, project concept reviews, and project pre-appraisal reports. Also, the long-term environmental effects may not have been noticeable at the time the project (or the loan disbursement) was completed. Environmental effects may emerge long after loan disbursement has been completed.
4. The potential positive effects of Bank lending were compromised by a number of factors:
   a. Policy recommendations were difficult in implement in practice.
   b. There was little guidance for selecting and designing projects.
   c. Recommendations were provided at a scale that was inadequate for sustainable development.
   d. The guiding ESW did not provide a comprehensive overview of developments in the country, and the activities of other multilateral and bilateral agencies were not considered.

These lessons provide scope for improving the design and cross-sectoral synergy in future investments for SLM and NRM. The following can serve as best-practice guidelines:

1. Incorporate newly available methods to assess synergies and tradeoffs via environmental impact assessments and resource baselines in problem assessments and subsequent project design, implementation, and monitoring.
2. Use currently available geographic information systems (GIS) to assemble relevant data layers (biophysical, economic, environmental, infrastructure, political, and social) at site, watershed, and landscape levels and couple these geo-referenced data layers with robust modeling to assess the effects of spatial and temporal factors.
3. Use the multisectoral GIS baseline described earlier to objectively assess the key SLM and NRM issues that need to be addressed in the short, medium, and long terms, and use this information to design and phase investments. Such an approach will reduce the likelihood of the flawed opportunistic investments identified by the OED evaluation in future SLM and NRM programs.
4. As highlighted in the previous sections, SLM interventions can have major cross-sector (land, forest, water, and biodiversity) implications. It is essential that project teams include members with competencies in these disciplines when investments are being planned and designed.
5. There is significant scope for leveraging GEF grant funds and carbon sequestration funds to facilitate the integration of global environmental (public good) issues in SLM and NRM programs that target agriculture and forestry sectors.

CHAPTER SIX

SLM: Strategic Options

Sustainable land management is vital for enhancing and sustaining the productivity of food and fiber systems globally. The world's highly productive grain, livestock, and forestry products systems need to be sustained and made more efficient in terms of reduced environmental impact. Where marginal lands have been occupied for agriculture and land degradation has occurred, there is an urgent need to stop further degradation and reverse the slide.

Though the specifics will vary from country to country and region to region, there are four main components to a comprehensive strategy for enhancing land productivity while countering degradation. These include:

- Policy and sector work
- Research and technology development
- Knowledge sharing and extension
- Providing incentives, expenditure priorities, and modes of financing

POLICY AND SECTOR WORK

Policy and sector work consists of aligning producer and consumer price incentives, fiscal and financial subsidies, licensing fees and taxation, and the structure of protection with a country's environmental and social policy objectives for SLM.

Land degradation, SLM, and poverty linkages need to be investigated further. Researchers in the global Alternatives to Slash and Burn (ASB) program developed a tool known as the ASB matrix (Tomich et al. 1998) to help policy makers assemble accurate, objective information regarding the private and social costs and benefits of alternative land use systems on which to base their research and adaptation efforts, as well as their inevitably controversial decisions.

In the ASB matrix, natural forest and the land use systems that replace it are scored against criteria reflecting the objectives of different interest groups. To enable results to be compared across sites, the systems specific to each site are grouped according to broad categories, ranging from agroforests to grasslands and pastures. See table 6.1 for indicators that can be fine-tuned for specific locations. This approach can readily be extended to a non–slash and burn environment involving common land use rights or hard-to-enforce private property rights.

RESEARCH AND TECHNOLOGY DEVELOPMENT

A revitalization of investments in agricultural and land use research will be needed to underpin the undertaking of SLM strategies and programs at the

Table 6.1 The ASB Matrix				
Meta land uses	Global environmental concerns	Agronomic sustainability	Smallholders' socioeconomic concerns	Policy and institutional issues
Natural forest				
Forest extraction				
Complex multistrata agroforestry systems				
Simple treecrop systems				
Crop or fallow systems				
Continuous annual cropping systems				
Grasslands or pasture				

Source: Tomich et al. 1998.

country and agroecological zone levels. Emphasis must be given to the adaptation and improvement of technologies associated with agricultural intensification, the management and rehabilitation of forest cover in sensitive watersheds, and more effective water management (to avert salinization and mitigate flooding) on irrigated and bottom lands.

A large number of studies have demonstrated that investments in agricultural research can produce significant returns (for instance, Gabre-Madhin and Haggblade 2004). Despite this evidence, however, current trends are not encouraging. In the wake of the generally successful "Green Revolution" of the 1970s and 1980s, support for institutes affiliated with the Consultative Group on International Agricultural Research (CGIAR) has fallen off sharply, as have fiscal and financial resource transfers to most national agricultural research systems and institutes (Timmer 2005). For example, African countries now spend only 0.5 percent of their agricultural GDP on research (Pardey and Beintema 2001).

Nonetheless, an important orientation for an adaptation agenda aimed toward SLM will be to identify and create cropping, animal, forest management, and on-farm water use systems that will benefit producers where it counts—in their pocketbooks—while serving the SLM objectives of, for example, land and soil conservation or the reversal of erosion, salinization, and other kinds of damage.

Several examples, at least partially successful, are available:

■ *Nutrient management and monitoring.* In Sub-Saharan Africa, during the past 10 years much attention has been focused on the quantification and estimation of nutrients that enter and leave agricultural systems. The balance between these nutrient inputs and outputs shows whether the agricultural system is a net gainer or a net loser of soil fertility. An FAO-commissioned mega-scale study (Stoorvogel and Smaling 1990) showed nitrogen, phosphorus, and potassium balances for land use systems in several countries, revealing that soil fertility in Africa is following a downward trend.[9]

  ■ Densely populated and hilly countries in the Rift Valley area (Kenya, Ethiopia, Rwanda, and Malawi) have the most negative values because of a high ratio of cultivated land to total arable land, relatively high crop yields, and soil erosion. The FAO-commissioned study triggered numerous case studies at plot, farm, and village levels of different degrees of sophistication. Some studies focused on the measurement of some flows, others on the linkage between nutrient balance and farm household economic performance, and others on participatory learning and action toward improving soil fertility and its management. The results have been published (for example, Buresh et al. 1997; Smaling 1998; Smaling et al. 1997; Scoones 2001; Tian et al. 2001; Vanlauwe et al. 2002) and have been integrated into a toolkit (NUTMON 2006).

- There have been few routine measurements of some potentially important nutrient flows (leaching, gaseous losses, and erosion) in the tropics, and their values are estimated. Accumulation of error renders the procedure vulnerable, but at the same time insight into the functioning of farming systems and agroecological zones as to soil fertility dynamics has increased significantly. Current knowledge gaps (apart from the difficult-to-measure flows) include the importance of crop-livestock integration and the kind of livestock system involved, dust input in West Africa, the potential of aquaculture as a source and a sink of nutrients, and the extent of periurban, nutrient exchange, that is, the classic win-win case of sanitation in town plus soil fertility around the town. The availability of high-precision, remote-sensing tools and GIS now allows a more precise disaggregation of the micro (plot), meso (region), and macro (country) scales, thereby greatly enhancing the precision of predictions (Schlecht and Hiernaux 2004).[10]

- *Conducting adaptive research on nutrients and seed.* This research was the foundation underlying the "starter pack" program in Malawi (Blackie and Mann 2005). Though the program ultimately failed, owing to the onset of a crippling drought and a hasty scaling-up by the government to serve essentially short-term political objectives, its design and the intended process of adaptation and farmer use were quite sound and offer several useful pointers. With the participation of the International Center for Maize and Wheat Improvement (CIMMYT) from the very start, the starter pack program aimed both to adapt CIMMYT's high-yielding hybrid maize varieties to Malawian growing conditions and to breed in the flinty texture favored by Malawi's households. It further sought to provide levels of fertilizer application consonant with maximization of farmers' net income rather than maximizing yields and prouction, which most of the country's smallholders simply could not afford. A third objective was rural poverty alleviation, which was to be accomplished by targeting the state's delivery system (seeds, fertilizers, and advice) at small farmers. The expectation was that, following the introduction of the starter packets more or less free of charge into Malawi's maize-growing areas, farmers would be willing to pay for the packets in subsequent seasons once the yield enhancements and real income benefits had become apparent. Because the adaptation effort lacked (by and large) the in-country financial and staff capabilities to conduct adaptive research, the involvement of CIMMYT was essential to that effort in Malawi, as well as to the design of the government's outreach and extension efforts. Thus, this effort shows the potential benefit of harnessing support from CGIAR institutions for the adaptation of "land-friendly" farming technologies, in collaboration with in-country resources.

- *Improving agricultural water management.* In recent years, there have been major advances in improving crop water productivity, irrigation efficiency, and management of evapotranspiration. The reader is referred to two important publications that detail these advances: *Reengaging in Agricultural Water Management: Challenges and Options* (World Bank 2006b) and *Shaping the*

Future of Water for Agriculture: A Sourcebook for Investment in Agricultural Water Management (World Bank 2005).

- *Public-private sector partnerships for farm inputs (nutrients and seed).* An example of such a partnership is the Farm Input Promotions Africa (FIPS-Africa) which involves private sector collaboration with public sector research and extension agencies in Kenya. The private sector partners include agribusiness firms (Monsanto, Dow Chemical), national seed companies and suppliers, and Athi River Mining (ARM), which produces a fertilizer called Mavuno, a fast-acting NPK fertilizer, enriched with micro-nutrients, sulfur, calcium, and magnesium, that is ideal for vegetables and cereals as well as for commercial crops like coffee, wheat, and tobacco. This fertilizer is made available, through local dealers, in small quantities (1–10 kg). In the Siaya and Busia districts of Western Kenya, total fertilizer use by collaborating farmers rose from 0 to 500 tons during a five-year period. Sales of 5- to 10-kg bags made up at least a quarter of all sales in many outlets. Some 40% of fertilizer sales were to women, and most customers were 20 years old or over (Seward and Okello 1998). FIPS has now moved beyond seed and fertilizer into helping farmers evaluate other important technologies—to reduce crop losses through treatment of crops in storage, and to improve weeding efficiency through herbicide application.

- *Introducing stress-tolerant crops and trees.* Plant breeders are making significant progress in developing new varieties that are better able to withstand both biotic (pests) and abiotic (for example, drought) stresses. The availability of crop varieties able to adapt and be productive under climate change scenarios will be especially important to minimize risk for poor rural farmers.

- *Rehabilitating degraded lands.* A priority is the rehabilitation of the productive and service functions of approximately 20 million hectares of degraded pasturelands in Brazil and more than 200 million hectares of deforested and degraded former croplands that are currently occupied by *Imperata cyclindrica–alang alang* in Southeast Asia and spear grass in West Africa. The hillsides of Central America and Southeast Asia, where soil erosion and nutrient mining has significantly reduced the productive capacity of the land and its resilience to storms, are also a priority. Agricultural and urban expansion into wetlands and coastal mangroves has severely compromised the flood protection provided by these lands. The devastating effect of the recent tsunamis along deforested coastlines in Asia and the flooding of New Orleans by Hurricane Katrina are but two examples of the effects of the degradation and loss of riparian and coastal forests, wetlands, and sediment banks, and their protective functions against wind and storm surges.

KNOWLEDGE SHARING AND EXTENSION

When promoting better land use practices, it will be important to build farmer innovation into national extension programs and into agricultural and natural resource management initiatives. Experience shows that farmers do not wait passively for extension advice, but actively experiment and innovate with agricultural and natural resource management practices. Their creativity may be one of the major underexploited resources in the Africa region (Reij and Waters-Bayer 2001; Mutunga and Critchley 2002).

A major advantage of innovations by farmers is that they are site-specific and often are readily acceptable to neighboring farmers. The incorporation of the farmer innovation approach within a systematic venue can significantly improve the performance of agroextension and technoadvisory services, particularly in the field of soil and water conservation, where the visual impact of demonstrations can be a powerful way to attract potential end users of "best practices." Although land users can financially contribute to costs, public funding will be required in the poorer areas to prepare and facilitate such visits and provide follow-up. Central to this will be the establishment of research partnerships to help farmers conserve their land and water resources and meet other environmental and social objectives. Advising and assisting agriculturalists in this area might be commercially unattractive for private companies,[11] but it should be an important role for the public sector.

Policy research is also needed to guide and support technological change. It should cover such questions as intellectual property rights, biosafety, and food safety. The need to better explain technological developments to consumers, farmers, and others in society is also critically important, as demonstrated by the public concern about and distrust of many improved crop varieties developed via biotechnology-mediated advances in plant breeding, for example, genetically modified varieties. Early attention to biosafety (human health and environmental impact) issues by those developing the technologies and transparent access to accurate and reliable information for end users of the technology is therefore important to facilitate the smooth introduction of new technologies.

Objective criteria are essential for analysis and management of the risks of new technology used for SLM and environmental protection. The opinions of the scientific community are frequently sought, but scientists are often absent from the public debate. In the future, it might help if researchers were encouraged to become much more involved in the knowledge dissemination and extension-outreach activities.

When designing extension programs (privately operated or public sector) and the feedback systems that can capture farmer innovation, consideration should be given to establishing regional centers where information on best practices or success stories can be accessed by farmers' organizations and others. Such an approach is especially important in the larger countries and in those with an agroecologically diverse natural resource endowment, where a "one-size-fits-all" approach does not work and innovative technologies need to be adapted to local conditions.

GIS and other technologies are central to achieving a successful transition from traditional environmental and resource management practices to sustainable development because of their integrative quality (linking social, economic, and environmental data) and place-based quality (addressing relationships among places at local, national, regional, and global levels).

For instance, there is a growing recognition by decision makers that problems at the intersection of agriculture and environmental management, climate change, and land cover change, with their attendant social and economic consequences, will be at the forefront in the new century. Technological advances fostering the integration of satellite imagery with other data (such as socioeconomic or health data) in GIS are opening new ways to synthesize complex and diverse geographic data sets, creating new opportunities for collaboration among natural and social scientists and decision makers at all levels.

Nonetheless, investments are urgently needed to overcome the following constraints on the effective use of GIS for improved SLM:

- Technical limitations of accessibility to data, such as inadequate telecommunications infrastructure, limited bandwidth, and low Internet connectivity.
- Administrative challenges of accessibility to data, including the inability of government officials to satisfy requests for information because of lack of familiarity with the subject matter, a shortage of efficient protocols for requesting government data, a lack of common and data standards to promote sharing, and a vexing array of unresolved issues of copyright and distribution.
- The inability to finance the collection and processing of needed data in many countries, especially those facing severe hard currency constraints.
- Educational and organizational limitations on access to data and technology, including a poorly trained workforce and limited private sector demand to spur the development of geographic information and tools.

The development of conserving technologies for land use, their adaptation to local environments, and the knowledge and diffusion elements of SLM strategy are very important components. Indeed, the more vexing problems associated with remedial measures for land degradation and soil conservation involve the lack of financially viable technical options that might encourage the undertaking of less destructive farming and logging practices. These more destructive practices are generally associated with unclear land use rights,[12] with poorly specified rights to manage public lands (thereby resulting in the so-called problem of the commons), or simply with corruption and inadequate enforcement.

The relative importance of the previously mentioned constraints to sustainable land management will vary from country to country, legal tradition to legal tradition, and even among jurisdictions within countries with people of diverse ethnicities, or where the laws, regulations, and rules of contract governing land rights and transfers of usufruct are themselves in the midst of transition and (re-)articulation (*viz.* China and the former Soviet Union). Thus, no simple menu of palliatives can be recommended to policy makers whose goal is to strengthen a country's SLM capabilities by addressing empty boxes in local legal tradition, short of saying that something can and usually should be done to rectify these shortcomings.

PROVIDING INCENTIVES, EXPENDITURE PRIORITIES, AND MODES OF FINANCING

In addition to incentives policies, normally operating at price and cost margins to redirect the private sector's utilization of resources in directions deemed socially desirable, achieving SLM will require investments in physical infrastructure, land reclamation and stabilization, replenishment of soil nutrients, and the replanting of tree cover. Additionally, improved forest management will normally be required.

The costs of these investments can be considerable in countries where severe degradation has already taken place, often over decades and even centuries (table 5.2 provides examples of actual Bank investments in WSM programs across the different regions). Thus, governments will need to (a) realistically assess the availability of resources, domestic and foreign; then (b) prioritize investments to rehabilitate the most egregiously damaged lands and soils (as measured, primarily, by the opportunity costs of taking no action); (c) develop a realistic phasing of investments; (d) set forth financing plans; and (e) seek agreements with likely beneficiaries in the private sector and civil society, both to participate in program implementation and to share a portion of the costs in accord with agreed mechanisms. To stimulate the involvement of private investors in land-friendly commercial activities would relieve pressures on the budget for adequate program finance while bringing to bear some of the flexibility and responsiveness needed to address the physical and financial contingencies associated with the above kinds of investments. The use of risk or guarantee funds or the provision of insurance, partially underwritten by government, might prove sufficient in some countries to induce a strong private-sector response.

For example, the International Finance Corporation (IFC) has recently contributed to a Chilean private equity forest fund (the Lignum Fund) that provides forest-backed securitization as an alternative captial market funding source for the forestry sector. At the same time, the fund will have an important environmental impact through sustainable forestry management practices and the afforestation of dry, eroded land that currently has marginal alternative agricultural use.

RECOMMENDED APPROACH AND THE ROLE OF THE WORLD BANK GROUP

The combination of regional and country experiences and examples from table 5.2 will likely weigh large in the selection of policies and instruments by governments that intend to place SLM high on their strategic agendas. In many cases, the shift from excessive resource consumption to a more ecologically sustainable land management profile will impose short-term costs on producers as well as consumers. In the Sub-Saharan uplands, the Andes highlands, and the piedmont and transmontane zones of South and East Asia, it is likely that very few households can afford to absorb sudden and substantial increases in the cost of living. An immediate implication is that economic growth will likely continue to require increased use of natural resources, at least in the short to medium term, leading to more resource degradation and misuse. However, this should not be considered a cause for inaction or despair. The lead time for many kinds of SLM inventions to pay off can be quite long, which mandates that remedial measures be initiated as quickly as possible, especially in the more seriously degraded watersheds and agroecological zones.

The Need for Phasing

Most countries—indeed, the world at large—probably could not sustain a broad-based attack on land and soil issues, even were the associated private costs of financing deemed politically acceptable. There will be a need for phasing, which underscores the related need to establish program and financing priorities.

Information Needs

While policy makers have devoted considerable attention to pollution issues and biodiversity in the past two decades, with full support from the international community, relatively less attention has been given to the technical and financial requisites of SLM. For example, many of the country environmental assessments offer only token proposals to reverse land degradation in damaged watersheds, and even fewer in support of soil conservation needs. In several countries, there is a need to fill yawning gaps in the available information concerning land quality and land use in the more fragile parts of the ecosystem. The systematic completion (or updating) of country-level and regional "watershed inventories," replete with technical data on land use and capabilities and on the severity of damage to lands and soils—including prospects for regeneration, as well as relevant socioeconomic data and indicators—would be a good place to begin.

Defining SLM Priorities

On the basis of more complete information and assessments of land use and land capability, policy makers, their advisors, and representatives of groups using land, water, or forest resources, as well as civil society, could debate and hopefully establish agreed priorities for SLM. The next steps would be to (a) match the agreed priorities with a supporting array of incentives policies and expenditure programs, (b) determine the respective roles of the private and public sectors in both program execution and the provision of requisite technical and financial support for implementation, and (c) adopt a phasing plan. Should external advisory assistance be required, ample grant funds and low-cost credits are available from bilateral and multilateral donors for technical assistance and training. Indeed, governments are well advised to actively seek this kind of assistance, because it comes replete with program advice and sometimes with an implied commitment to help finance start-up initiatives.

Role of the Bank and the Global Environment Facility (GEF)

The Bank Group (including GEF) can play an important role in jump starting SLM initiatives worldwide. It either has, or can quickly mobilize, both the often-needed advisory capabilities and implementation financing. Additionally, the Bank Group is organized as a center for knowledge exchange, which can be especially useful to governments intending to adopt more land-sustaining approaches toward development.

Since its establishment in 1991, the GEF has been providing incremental funding to assist countries to prevent and control land degradation, primarily desertification and deforestation, as it relates to its four focal areas (biodiversity conservation, climate change, international waters, and ozone layer depletion). To further improve the GEF's assistance for land degradation prevention and control, the GEF Council recommended the designation of land degradation as a focal area, as a means to enhance GEF support for the successful implementation of the United Nations Convention to Combat Desertification (UNCCD). This designation makes sustainable land management a primary focus of GEF assistance.

From 2003 to 2006, the GEF allocated a total of $500 million to support land degradation prevention and control activities—$250 million under the sustainable land management focal area and another $250 million for activities within other focal areas—biodiversity conservation, climate change, international waters, and persistent organic pollutants. In addition, GEF facilitating country partnership programs on sustainable land management aimed at assisting GEF-eligible countries to address land degradation issues in a comprehensive and integrated manner based on priorities outlined in their National Action Plans (NAPs) on Desertification and Poverty Reduction Strategy Papers (PRSPs). The partnership will comprise a package of interventions to address land degradation policy, regulatory and institutional reforms, capacity building, and investments financed, in a coordinated way, from a variety of sources, including national budgets, bilateral development cooperation agreements, country assistance programs of multilateral agencies, and private foundations.

The success of the Bank's endeavor to generate country-managed environmental assessments as a requisite for CAS approval, and the Bank and fund's support for poverty-reduction strategy programs (PRSPs), including the positive outcomes of these exercises, suggests that a similar approach should be followed to promote borrowers' commitment to SLM. Allowing that many of the Bank's clients are probably experiencing a degree of "assessment fatigue," the effort should perhaps be initially aimed at the regional level by selecting a subset of willing countries within each region to carry out land use and land degradation assessments and then arrange to conduct these with assistance mobilized by the Bank or GEF. The expected outcome, of course, will be the articulation of SLM action programs, including timetables and financing plans. The involvement of the regional development banks, the European Union, bilateral donors, and even United Nations agencies at this early stage might broaden the appeal of the approach.

Once initial country plans have been articulated and design and implementation efforts have commenced, the demonstration effect will likely make it possible to entice other countries to carry out SLM assessments. After all, these pilots can likely demonstrate that international funds will be forthcoming should a government's effort appear adequate and properly focused.

The Bank's regions differ markedly, and there is no "one-size-fits-all" approach that will be likely to result in the successful introduction of SLM. Unlike the PRSPs and the earlier environmental assessments, the specificity of land use policies in most countries strikes close to the heart of rural livelihoods and powerful business interests. For the regional vice presidencies that choose to move forward quickly, pilot demonstration and technical assistance in willing countries could be incorporated into ongoing CAS. But generally, a more measured approach might be required to induce serious response. This study thus recommends, as an initial step, that regional workshops be organized to highlight the need, modalities, and practicality of SLM-type interventions and the long-term (and somewhat catastrophic) consequences for humans of failing to do so. In parallel, the resources available to GEF, the Global Development Learning Network, and the World Bank Institute could be harnessed to spread the message electronically, while conferences and symposia could be organized to intensify the debate over land-conserving priorities, as well as to link the findings of ongoing research with the SLM message(s) staff wish to convey. For example, to promote South-South learning on practical issues related to SLM and reduced environmental degradation, the WBI recently organized a GDLN event to share China's experience on poverty reduction on fragile land with African countries that are facing similar land and environmental degradation problems.

In 2005, countries such as Bhutan, Cameroon, Kenya, Madagascar, Mozambique, and the Philippines have undertaken dedicated SLM investments with IDA and GEF resources. The goal of such investments is to improve local SLM benefits and livelihoods and to harness the synergies with global environment benefits. These are promising developments and could prove catalytic for additional and similar investments elsewhere.

Land Management and a Useful Plant Diversity Index ("V" Index)

A generic rapid survey protocol for measuring plant biodiversity according to richness in species and plant functional types has been developed and applied in a number of ecoregional baseline studies along a series of land use intensity gradients in the Congo Basin (Cameroon), India, Thailand, Sumatra, and the Amazon Basin (Brazil and Peru). Typical baselines include vegetation types ranging along land use intensity gradients from relatively intact forest to secondary growth; agro-forests; plantations; agricultural fallow sequences, including slash and burn, mixed cropping, and mono-cropping; to improved and degraded pasture. The sampling protocol also includes vegetation structure and key site physical features. When used in multitaxon baseline studies, high correlations are invariably found between subsets of these variables and certain groups of fauna. The best overall subset of plant-based predictors comprises richness in species and plant functional type (PFT), a species-to-PFT ratio, mean canopy height, and basal area of all woody plants.

When subjected to multidimensional scaling, a single best eigenvector score for these five variables can be obtained for any data set. By ranking the scores between 1 and 10, a relative numeric index can be attached to any one of the land use types under investigation. Although the index is not specifically a "biodiversity" index, the combination of species and PFT richness, together with key elements of vegetation structure, provides an empirical, integrated measure of plant diversity. The V index derived from this integrated procedure has been found to be empirically useful as a means of ranking land use types in each of the previously mentioned ecoregional baseline studies (figure A1.1).

Figure A1.1   Relationship between Land Use Type, Plant Biodiversity,
and Oil Palm Tenure, Jambi, Sumatra

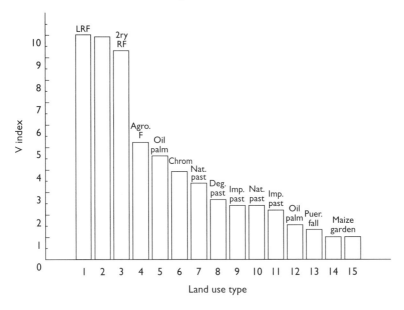

Source: Gillison 2000.
Legend: LRF: Rainforest; 2ryRF: Secondary forest; Agro. F: Agroforestry; Chrom: *Chromolaena odorata;* Nat. past: Native pasture; Deg. past: Degraded pasture; Imp. past: Improved pasture; Puer. fall: Pueraria fallow.

As such, it provides a potentially useful numeric vegetation-based surrogate for resource analysis.

Although V indexes are purely a function of the data set under study, for typical ecoregional gradients ranging from forest to degraded grassland, index values of between 5 and 8 tend to reflect "best bet" practices for sustainable land management. These typically include agroforests and secondary forests enriched with crops such as rubber and cacao. These values tend to be consistent across similar land use types in different countries and raise the possibility of their use as a numerical basis for comparative economic valuation of biodiversity. Apart from their indicator value within regional landscapes, indexes have been shown to be useful predictors of biodiversity in particular land management types (figure A1.2). In Sumatra, a V index is highly correlated with above-ground carbon and certain soil variables, thus providing a nexus between above-ground carbon, biodiversity, and potential agricultural productivity. From a socioeconomic perspective, the V index shows promise as an indicator of profitability (total factor profitability) and employment (see figure A1.3) and has been used to detect differences in cropping under differing land tenures.

Figure A1.2   Relationship between Land Use Type, Plant Biodiversity, and
Age of Oil Palm Plantation, Jambi District, Sumatra (Indonesia)

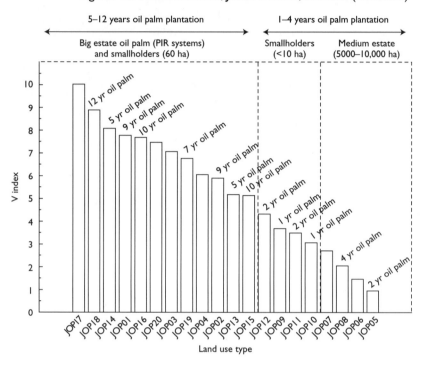

Figure A1.3   Relationship between Employment and Plant Biodiversity,
Jambi, Sumatra

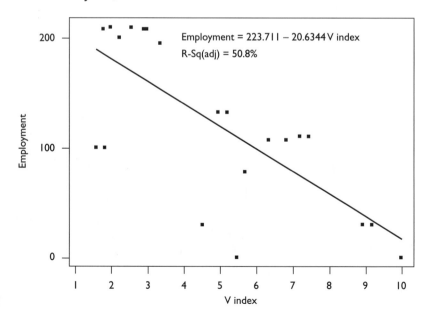

1. Numerous definitions of sustainable agriculture and natural resource management exist (Crosson and Anderson 1993; Smyth and Dumanski 1993; Hurni et al. 1996) that are equally applicable to land management. This report draws upon these in the definition provided earlier.

2. Overdesigned irrigation systems, inadequate drainages, secondary and rural roads with insufficient culverts, and expansion of villages and village infrastructure much too far into the uplands or into fragile agroecological zones (for example, the former Soviet Union and China).

3. The FAO (2000) estimates for developing countries show that, over the past four decades, the amount of land under agriculture has increased to around 1 billion hectares, although the amount of cultivated cropland per capita has declined by almost a half since 1960. The area under pasture increased by about 15 percent, to 2.2 billion hectares, mostly via expansion into rainforests and savanna woodlands. The total irrigated land in developing countries has doubled since the 1960s, to around 197 million hectares. Irrigated agriculture currently consumes roughly 70 percent of the world's fresh water used by humans.

4. Though it can also be argued that the damage has already been done in other regions, that it is both historical and irreversible.

5. Pagiola (1999) suggests, however, that the poverty–land degradation relationship is unlikely to be unambiguous and is not as simple as is often assumed. The author suggests that the assertions that the poor tend to conserve less and degrade more are little more than "plausible hypotheses" based on assumed characteristics of the poor, and that these same assumed characteristics could easily lead to a plausible hypothesis that the poor conserve more and degrade less.

6. The change in land management approaches to reduce the risk of climate change also is referred to as "adaptation." The definition of *adaptation* used here is that of Smit et al. (1999, 2000) and of the IPCC (2001): *adaptation* refers to the "adjustment

in ecological, social, or economic systems in response to actual or expected climatic stimuli and their effects or impacts." The term *adaptation* refers to changes in "processes, practices, or structures to moderate or offset potential damages or to take advantage of opportunities associated with changes in climate" (IPCC 2001). Adaptation involves adjustments to decrease the vulnerability of communities and regions to climate change and variability (IPCC 2001). As an interesting aside, Adger and Kelly (2001) view adaptation as a dynamic social process and believe that the ability of a society to act collectively determines its ability to adapt.

7. Country-level research is needed to identify investments and institutions, both public and private, that can reduce costs and risks and provide incentives for the adoption of improved production, processing, and marketing technology throughout the food system (Kelly et al. 1999).

8. IBRD IDA grants and GEF grants.

9. Using a nutrient balance model, Stoorvogel and Smaling (1990) calculated that, on average, 660 kilograms of nitrogen per hectare, 75 kilograms of phosphorus per hectare, and 450 kilograms of potassium per hectare have been lost during the past 30 years from about 200 million hectares of land in 37 African countries, primarily in crop harvests. This amounts to annual losses of about 8 million tons of nitrogen, phosphorus, and potassium. Stoorvogel and Smaling (1990) concluded that no systems can sustain such large net imbalances between nutrient acquisition and losses, so restoration of fertility, let alone enhancement of crop yield, requires substantial nutrient inputs in the form of organic materials or commercial fertilizers.

10. However, their fundamental conclusion remains unchanged: that soil fertility in Sub-Saharan Africa continues to decline.

11. Unless organized under the umbrella of longer-term service agreements, perhaps with some subsidization and with assurance by private service providers that contracts will be honored and enforced and that payments will be received more or less routinely. Armenia's animal breeding and animal health services provide good examples of how private sector services can be mobilized successfully, partly financed by the public sector.

12. Whether ensconced in the exercise of private freehold or conveyed by indirect tenure (i.e., leasing, share rental, and the like) or by concessions, licensing, and other kinds of permissions granted to identified users by public authority.

BIBLIOGRAPHY

Adger, W. N., and P. M. Kelly. 2001. "Social vulnerability and resilience." In *Living with Environmental Change: Social Vulnerability, Adaptation and Resilience in Vietnam,* ed. W. N. Adger, P. M. Kelly, and Nhuyen Huu Ninh, 19–34. London: Routledge.

Anderson, J. R., and J. Thampapillai. 1990. *Soil Conservation in Developing Countries: Project and Policy Intervention.* Policy and Research Series 8. Washington, DC: World Bank.

Angelsen, A., and D. Kaimowitz. 2001. "When Does Technological Change in Agriculture Promote Deforestation?" In *Tradeoffs or Synergies: Agricultural Intensification, Economic Development and the Environment,* ed. D. R. Lee and C. B. Barrett, 89–114. Wallingford, UK: CABI.

Ashby, J. 1985. "Women and Agricultural Technology in Latin America and the Carribbean." Background document prepared for a seminar of the Center on Women and Agricultural Technology, Bellagio, Italy, March 25–29. Inter-American Development Bank (IADB).

Aylward, B., J. Echeverría, A. F. González, I. Porras, K. Allen, and R. Mejías. 1998. *Economic Incentives for Watershed Protection: A Case Study of Lake Arenal, Costa Rica.* Final Report. London: International Institute for Environment and Development, Tropical Science Center, San José, Costa Rica; International Center in Economic Policy, National University, Heredia, Costa Rica. February.

Baland, J. M., and J. P. Platteau. 1996. *Halting Degradation of Natural Resources: Is There a Role for Rural Communities?* Oxford: Oxford University Press.

Bekele, S., and S. T. Holden. 1999. "Soil Erosion and Smallholders' Conservation Decisions in the Highlands of Ethiopia." *World Development* 27 (4): 739–52.

Benin, S. 2005. "Policies and Programs Affecting Land Management Practices, Input Use and Productivity in the Highlands of Amhara Region, Ethiopia. In *Strategies for Sustainable Land Management in the East African Highlands,* ed. J. Pender, F. Place, and S. Ehui. Washington, DC: International Food Policy Research Institute.

Binswanger, H., Y. Mundlak, M. C. Yang, and A. Bowers. 1987. "On the Determinants of Cross-Country Aggregate Agricultural Supply." *Journal of Econometrics* 36: 111–31.

Blackie, M., and C. Mann. 2005. "The Origin and Concept of the Starter Pack." In *Starter Packs: A Strategy to Fight Hunger in Developing Countries,* ed. S. Levy. Wallingford, UK: CABI.

Blaikie, P., and H. Brookfield, eds. 1987. *Land Degradation and Society.* London and New York: Methuen.

Bojo, J. 1996. "The Costs of Land Degradation in Sub-Saharan Africa." *Ecological Economics* 16: 161–73.

Bruce, J. W., and R. Mearns. 2004. *Natural Resource Management and Land Policy in Developing Countries: Lessons Learned and New Challenges for the World Bank.* Washington, DC: World Bank.

Buresh, R. J., P. A. Sanchez, and F. Calhoun, eds. 1997. *Replenishing Soil Fertility in Africa.* Madison, WI: Soil Science Society of America Special Publication No. 51.

Burton, I., and M. van Aalst. 2004. *Look before You Leap: A Risk Management Approach for Incorporating Climate Change Adaptation in World Bank Operations.* Washington, DC: World Bank.

Calder, I. R. 1998. *Water-Resource and Land-Use Issues.* Systemwide Initiative on Water Management (SWIM). Paper No. 3. Colombo: International Water Management Institute.

———. 2005. *The Blue Revolution: Land Use and Integrated Water Resource Management.* Second Edition. London: Earthscan.

Carret, J.C., and D. Loyer. 2003. "Madagascar Protected Area Network Sustainable Financing: Economic Analysis Perspective." Paper contributed to the World Park's Congress, Durban, South Africa, September.

Chomitz, K. M., E. Brenes, and L. Constantino. 1998. "Financing Environmental Services: The Costa Rican Experience and Its Implications." Paper prepared for Development Research Group (DRG) and Environmentally and Socially Sustainable Development—Latin America and Caribbean (ESSD-LCR). World Bank, Washington, DC.

Cromwell, E., P. Kambewa, R. Mwanza, and R. Chirwa. 2001. "Impact Assessment Using Participatory Approaches: 'Starter Pack' and Sustainable Agriculture in Malawi." Network Paper No. 112. London: Overseas Development Institute (ODI) / Agricultural Research and Extension Network (AGREN).

Crosson, P., and J. R. Anderson. 1993. "Concerns for Sustainability: Integration of Natural Resource and Environmental Issues for the Research Agendas of NARSs." Research Report No. 4. The Hague: International Service for National Agricultural Research (ISNAR).

Deininger, K., and B. Minten. 1996. "Poverty, Policies, and Deforestation: The Case of Mexico. Research Project on Social and Environmental Consequences of Growth-Oriented Policies." Working Paper No. 5. World Bank Policy Research Department, Washington, DC.

Desanker, P. V., P. G. H. Frost, C. O. Frost, C.O. Justice, and R. J. Scholes, eds. 1997. *The Miombo Network: Framework for a Terrestrial Transect Study of Land-Use and Land-Cover Change in the Miombo Ecosystems of Central Africa.* IGBP Report 41. Stockholm: International Geosphere-Biosphere Programme (IGBP). 109 p.

Dewees, P. A. 1996. "The Miombo Woodlands of Southern Africa: Emerging Priorities and Common Themes for Dryland Forest management." *Commonwealth Forestry Review* 75 (2): 130–35.

Dixon, J., A. Gulliver, and D. Gibbon. 2001. *Farming Systems and Poverty: Improving Farmers' Livelihoods in a Changing World.* Rome and Washington, DC: FAO and the World Bank.

Dobie, P. 2001. *Poverty and Drylands.* Nairobi, Kenya. The Global Dry Lands Partnership.

Dorward, A., J. Kydd, J. Morrison, and I. Urey. 2004. "A Policy Agenda for Pro-Poor Agricultural Growth." *World Development* 32 (1): 73–89.

Enters, T. E. 1998. *Methods for the Economic Assessment of the On- and Off-Site Impacts of Soil Erosion.* Issues in Sustainable Land Management No. 2. Bangkok: International Board for Soil Research and Management.

Evenson, R. E., and D. Gollin. 2003. "Assessing the Impact of the Green Revolution, 1960 to 2000." *Science,* 2 May: 758–62.

Falkenmark, M., W. Klohn, J. Lundqvist, S. Postel, J. Rockström, D. Seckler, H. Shuval, and J. Wallace. 1998. "Water Scarcity as a Key Factor behind Global Food Insecurity: Round Table Discussion." *Ambio* 27 (2).

Fan, S., and P. Hazell. 1997. "Should India Invest More in Less-Favored Areas?" EPTD Discussion Paper No. 25. International Food Policy Research Institute, Washington, DC.

FAO (Food and Agriculture Organization). 1995. *TAC Study on Priorities and Strategies for Soil and Water Aspects of Natural Resource Management Research in the CGIAR.* Rome: FAO.

———. 1999. *Expert Consultation on Soil and Nutrient Management in SSA, in Support of the Soil Fertility Initiative (SFI): Summary Report, Conclusions, and Recommendations.* Rome: FAO.

———. 2000. *Crops and Drops: Making the Best Use of Land and Water.* Rome: FAO.

———. 2003. *World Agriculture: Towards 2015/2030, an FAO Perspective.* London: FAO/ Earthscan.

———. 2005. *Agro-Ecological Zoning and GIS Applications in Asia, with Special Emphasis on Land Degradation Assessment in Drylands (LADA): Proceedings of a Regional Workshop.* Bangkok, Thailand, November 10–14, 2003. Rome: FAO. 125 p.

FAOSTAT. 2004. http://faostat.fao.org/default.jsp. Accessed November.

Feder, G., R. Murgai, and J. B. Quizon. 2003. "Sending Farmers Back to School: The Impact of Farmer Field Schools in Indonesia." *Review of Agricultural Economics* 26: 45–62.

Fernandes, E. C. M., P. P. Motavalli, C. Castilla, and L. Mukurumbira. 1997. "Management Control of Soil Organic Matter Dynamics in Tropical Land Use Systems." *Geoderma* 79: 49–67.

Fernandes, E. C. M., E. Wandelli, R. Perin, and S. A. Garcia. 2006. "Restoring Productivity to Degraded Pasture Lands in the Amazon through Agroforestry Practices." In *Biological Approaches to Sustainable Soil Systems,* ed. N. Uphoff, A. Ball, E. Fernandes, H. Herren, O. Husson, M. Laing, C. Palm, J. Pretty, P. Sanchez, N. Sanginga, and J. Thies, 305–18. New York: CRC Press.

FRP (Forestry Research Programme). 2005. "From the Mountain to the Tap: How Land Use and Water Management Can Work for the Rural Poor." Report of a dissemination project funded by the United Kingdom Department for International Development (DFID) for the benefit of developing countries. Forestry Research Programme, NR International Ltd. Hayle, UK: Rowe The Printers.

Gabre-Madhin, E., and S. Haggblade. 2001. *Successes in African Agriculture: Results of an Expert Survey.* Washington, DC: International Food Policy Research Institute.

———. 2004. "Successes in African Agriculture: Results of an Expert Survey." *World Development* 32 (5): 745–66.

Geist, H. J., and E. F. Lambin. 2002. "Proximate Causes and Underlying Driving Forces of Tropical Deforestation." *BioScience* 52 (2): 143–50.

Gewin, V. 2002. "The State of the Planet." *Nature* 417: 112–13.

Gillison, A. N. 2000. "Rapid Vegetation Survey." In *Above-Ground Biodiversity Assessment Working Group Summary Report 1996–99: Impact of Different Land Uses on Biodiversity,* ed. A. N. Gillison, 25–38. Nairobi: Alternatives to Slash and Burn Project, International Center for Research in Agroforestry (ICRAF).

———. 2002. *Bioregional Assessment, Land Use and Zoning for Biodiversity Conservation in NW Mato Grosso: Baseline Survey for the Municipalities of Castanheira, Cotriguaçu and Juruena.* Report prepared for the United Nations Development Program / Global Environment Facility and PróNatura.

Gisladottir, G., and M. Stocking. 2005. "Land Degradation Control and Its Global Environmental Benefits." *Land Degradation and Development* 16: 99–112.

Grey, D., and C. Sadoff. 2002. "Water Resources and Poverty in Africa: Essential Economic and Political Responses." Paper presented at the African Ministerial Conference on Water, Abuja, Nigeria.

Herweg, K. 1993. "Problems of Acceptance and Adoption of Soil Conservation in Ethiopia." *Tropics Applied Resource Management* 3: 391–411.

Hope, R. A. 2005. "Water, Workfare and Poverty: The Impact of the Working for Water Programme on Rural Poverty Reduction." *Environment, Development and Sustainability.* FRP R7937.

Hurni, H. 1993. "Land Degradation, Famines, and Resources Scenarios in Ethiopia." In *World Soil Erosion and Conservation,* ed. D. Pimentel. Cambridge: Cambridge University Press.

Hurni, H., with the assistance of an international group of contributors. 1996. *Precious Earth: From Soil and Water Conservation to Sustainable Land Management.* Bern: International Soil Conservation Organisation (ISCO) and Centre for Development and Environment (CDE).

Ingram, J. S. I., and E. C. M. Fernandes. 2001. "Managing Carbon Sequestration in Soils: A Note on Concepts and Terminology." *Agriculture Ecosystems & the Environment* 87: 111–17.

IPCC (Intergovernmental Panel on Climate Change). 2001. *Climate Change 2001: The Scientific Basis.* Intergovernmental Panel on Climate Change. Cambridge: Cambridge University Press.

Keenan, R. J., M. Parsons, E. O'Loughlin, A. Gerrand, S. Beavis, D. Gunawardana, M. Gavran, and A. Bugg. 2004. "Plantations and Water Use: A Review." Forest and Wood Products Research and Development Corporation. Canberra, Australia: Bureau of Rural Sciences.

Kelly, V., A. Adesina, and A. Gordon. 2003. "Expanding Access to Agricultural Inputs in Africa: A Review of Recent Market Development Experience." *Food Policy* 28: 379–404.

Kelly, V. A., E. W. Crawford, J. A. Howard, T. Jayne, J. Staatz, and M. T. Weber. 1999. "Towards a Strategy for Improving Agricultural Input Markets in Africa." *Policy Synthesis.* Food Security II Cooperative Agreement, Michigan State University, Department of Agricultural Economics.

Meinzen-Dick, R. S., L. R. Brown, H. S. Feldstein, and A. R. Quisumbing. 1997. "Gender, Property Rights, and Natural Resources." *World Development* 25 (8): 1303–15.

Millennium Development Goals. http://www.developmentgoals.org. Accessed January 12.

MEA (Millennium Ecosystem Assessment). 2005a. *Ecosystems and Human Well-being: Synthesis.* Washington, DC: Island Press.

———. 2005b. *Ecosystems and Human Well-being: Desertification Synthesis.* Washington, DC: World Resources Institute.

Miranda, M., I. T. Porras, and M. Luz Moreno. 2003. *The Social Impacts of Payments for Environmental Services in Costa Rica: A Quantitative Field Survey and Analysis of the Virilla Watershed.* London: International Institute for Environment and Development.

Mittermeier, R. A., N. Myers, P. R. Gil, and C. Mittermeier. 1999. *Hotspots: Earth's Biologically Richest and Most Endangered Terrestrial Ecoregions.* Mexico City: Conservation International.

Mutunga, K., and W. Critchley. 2002. *Farmer's Initiatives in Land Husbandry.* Nairobi: Sida's Regional Land Management Unit, International Center for Research in Agroforestry (ICRAF).

Muller, D., and M. Zeller. 2002. "Land Use Dynamics in the Central Highlands of Vietnam: A Spatial Model Combining Village Survey Data with Satellite Imagery Interpretation." *Agricultural Economics* 27 (3): 333–54.

Newcombe, K. 2003. "Extending the Carbon Market to the World's Poor." Paper presented at the ABCDE Conference, Europe. Report No. 28732. World Bank, Washington, DC.

Nimlos, T. J., and R. F. Savage. 1991. "Successful Soil Conservation in the Ecuadorian Highlands." *Journal of Soil and Water Conservation* 46: 341–43.

NUTMON (Nutrient Monitoring for Tropical Farming Systems). 2006. Toolbox available for download. http://www.nutmon.org. Accessed April.

OECD (Organisation for Economic Co-operation and Development). 1993. "Environmental Indicators: Basic Concepts and Terminology." Background paper No. 1. OECD, Paris, 150 p.

Otsuka, K., and A. Quisumbing. 1998. "Gender and Forest Resource Management: A Synthesis of Case Studies in Ghana and Sumatra." In *Gender and Forest Resource Management: A Comparative Study in Selected Areas of Asia and Africa.* Washington, DC: International Food Policy Research Institute. Mimeo.

Pagiola, S. 1995. "Environmental and Natural Resource Degradation in Intensive Agriculture in Bangladesh." Paper No. 15, Environmental Economics Series. World Bank, Washington, DC. June.

———. 1996. "Price Policy and Returns to Soil Conservation in Semi-arid Kenya." *Environmental and Resource Economics* 8: 255–71.

———. 1999. "The Global Environmental Benefits of Land Degradation Control on Agricultural Land." Environment Paper 16. Global Overlays Program, World Bank, Washington, DC.

Pagiola, S., J. Bishop, and N. Landell-Mills. 2002. *Selling Forest Environmental Services: Market-Based Mechanisms for Conservation and Development.* London: Earthscan.

Pagiola, S., K. von Ritter, and J. Bishop J. 2004. "Assessing the Economic Value of Ecosystem Conservation." Environment Department Paper No. 101. World Bank Environment Department (Washington, DC) in collaboration with the Nature Conservancy and International Union for Conservation of Nature and Natural Resources (IUCN).

Pardey, P., and N. Beintema. 2001. *Slow Magic: Agricultural R&D a Century after Mendel.* Food Policy Report. Washington, DC: International Food Policy Research Institute.

Pearce, D. W., and J. J. Watford. 1993. *World without End*. New York: Oxford University Press.

Pender, J. 2004. "Development Pathways for Hillsides and Highlands: Some Lessons from Central America and East Africa." *Food Policy* 29: 339–67.

Pender, J., and B. Gebremedhin. 2004. "Impacts of Policies and Technologies in Dryland Agriculture: Evidence from Northern Ethiopia." In *Challenges and Strategies for Dryland Agriculture,* ed. S.C. Rao. Special Publication 32. Madison, WI: American Society of Agronomy and Crop Science Society of America.

Pichon, F. J. 1997. "Colonist Land-Allocation Decisions, Land Use, and Deforestation in the Ecuadorean Amazon Frontier." *Economic Development and Cultural Change* 44: 707–44.

Pieri, C., G. Evers, J. Landers, P. O'Connell, and E. Terry. 2002. "No-Till Farming for Sustainable Rural Development." ARD Working Paper. World Bank, Washington, DC.

Piha, M. I. 1993. "Optimizing Fertilizer Use and Practical Rainfall Capture in a Semi-arid Environment with Variable Rainfall." *Experimental Agriculture* 29: 405–15.

Reardon, T., and S. A. Vosti. 1992. "Issues in the Analysis of the Effects of Policy on Conservation and Productivity at the Household Level in Developing Countries." *Quarterly Journal of International Agriculture* 31 (4): 380–96.

———. 1995. "Links between Rural Poverty and the Environment in Developing Countries: Asset Categories and Investment Poverty." *World Development* 23 (9): 1495–1506.

Reij, C., and D. Steeds. 2003. *Success Stories in Africa's Drylands: Supporting Advocates and Answering Skeptics.* Rome: Global Mechanism of the United Nations Convention to Combat Desertification.

Reij, C., and A. Waters-Bayer. 2001. *Farmer Innovation in Africa: A Source of Inspiration for Agricultural Development.* London: Earthscan. 362 p.

Reij, C., I. Scoones, and C. Toulmin. 1996. *Indigenous Soil Conservation.* London: Earthscan.

Sanchez, P. A., K. D. Shepherd, M. J. Soule, F. M. Place, A. U. Mukwenye, R. J. Buresh, F. R. Kwesiga, A. Izac, C. G. Ndiritu, and P. L. Woomer. 1997. "Soil Fertility Replenishment in Africa: An Investment in Natural Resource Capital." In R. J. Buresh et al., eds., *Replenishing Soil Fertility in Africa,* 1–46. Special Publication No. 51. Madison, WI: Soil Science Society of America (SSSA).

Scherr, S. J., and P. A. Hazell. 1994. "Sustainable Agricultural Development Strategies in Fragile Lands." Environment and Production Technology Division (EPTD) Discussion Paper 1. International Food Policy Research Institute, Washington, DC.

Schlager, E., and E. Ostrom. 1992. "Property-Rights Regimes and Natural Resources: A Conceptual Analysis." *Land Economics* 68: 249–62.

Schlecht, E., and P. Hiernaux. 2004. "Beyond Adding Up Inputs and Outputs: Process Assessment and Upscaling in Modelling Nutrient Flows." *Nutrient Cycling in Agroecosystems* 70: 303–19.

Scholes, B. 1996. "Miombo Woodlands and Global Change." In *The Miombo in Transition: Woodlands and Welfare in Africa,* ed. B. Campbell, 13. Bogor: Center for International Forestry Research.

Scholes, R. J., and R. Biggs. 2004. *Ecosystem Services in Southern Africa: A Regional Perspective.* Pretoria: Council for Scientific and Industrial Research (CSIR).

Scoones, I. 1998. "Sustainable Rural Livelihoods: A Framework for Analysis." Working Paper No. 72. Institute for Development Studies, Brighton, England.

————. 2001. *Dynamics and Diversity: Soil Fertility and Farming Livelihoods in Africa.* London: Earthscan.

Scoones, I., and C. Toulmin. 1999. "Policies for Soil Fertility Management in Africa." Report prepared for the Department for International Development, London, by the Institute for Development Studies (IDS) and the International Institute for Environment and Development (IIED).

Seitz, W. D., R. C. Taylor, R. G. F. Spitze, C. Osteen, and M. C. Nelson. 1979. "Economic Impacts of Soil Erosion Control." *Land Economics* 55 (1): 28–42.

Seward, P., and D. Okello. 1998. "Methods to Develop an Infrastructure for the Supply of the Appropriate Fertilizers for Use by Small Farmers in Sub-Saharan Africa: Experience from Western Kenya." Paper presented at the IFA Regional Conference, Maputo, Mozambique, June 8–12 (mimeo).

Shively, G., and S. N. Pagiola. 2004. "Agricultural Intensification, Local Labor Markets, and Deforestation in the Philippines." *Environment and Development Economics* 9: 241–66.

SIWI (Stockholm International Water Institute), IFPRI (International Food Policy Research Institute), IUCN (International Union for Conservation of Nature and Natural Resources), and IWMI (International Water Management Institute). 2005. "Let It Reign: The New Water Paradigm for Global Food Security." Final Report to CSD-13. Stockholm International Water Institute, Stockholm.

Smaling, E. M. A., ed. 1998. "Nutrient Balances as Indicators of Productivity and Sustainability in Sub-Saharan African Agriculture." *Agriculture, Ecosystems & Environment* 71.

Smaling E. M. A., S. M. Nandwa, and B. H. Janssen. 1997. "Soil Fertility in Africa Is at Stake." In *Replenishing Soil Fertility in Africa.* R. J. Buresh et al., ed. Special Publication 51. Madison, WI: Soil Science Society of America (SSSA).

Smit, B., I. Burton, R. Klein, and T. Street. 1999. "The Science of Adaptation: A Framework for Assessment." *Mitigation and Adaptation Strategies for Global Change* 4: 199–213.

Smit, B., I. Burton, R. Klein, and J. Wandel. 2000. "The Anatomy of Adaptation to Climate Change and Variability." *Climatic Change* 45: 223–51.

Smyth, A. J., and J. Dumanski. 1993. "FESLM: An International Framework for Evaluating Sustainable Land Management: A Discussion Paper." World Soil Resources Report 73. Food and Agriculture Organization, Rome. 74 p.

Stoorvogel, J. J., and E. M. A. Smaling. 1990. "Assessment of Soil Nutrient Depletion in Sub-Sahara Africa: 1983–2000." Report 28. Winand Staring Centre for Integrated Land, Soil and Water Research, Wageningen, The Netherlands.

Templeton, S., and S. J. Scherr. 1997. "Population Pressure and the Microeconomy of Land Management in Hills and Mountains of Developing Countries." EPTD Discussion Paper No. 26. International Food Policy Research Institute, Washington, DC.

Thrupp, L. A. 1993. *Green Guidance for Latin America and the Caribbean.* Washington, DC: Bureau for Latin America and the Caribbean, United States Agency for International Development: Center for International Development and Environment, World Resources Institute.

————. 1998. *Cultivating Diversity: Agrobiodiversity and Food Security.* Washington, DC: World Resources Institute.

Thurston, D. H. 1997. *Slash/Mulch Systems: Sustainable Methods for Tropical Agriculture.* Boulder, Colorado: Westview Press.

Tian, H. D., T. Kumamaru, Y. Takemoto, M. Ogawa, and H. Satoh. 2001. "Gene Analysis of New 57H Mutant Gene, *glup6*, in Rice." *RGN* 18: 48–50.

Tiffen, M., and M. Mortimore. 1992. "Environment, Population Growth and Productivity in Kenya: A Case Study of Machakos District." *Development Policy Review* 10: 359–87

Tiffen, M., M. Mortimore, and F. Gichuki. 1994. *More People, Less Erosion: Environmental Recovery in Kenya.* Chichester, England: John Wiley and Sons.

Timmer, C. P. 2005. "Agriculture and Pro-Poor Growth: An Asian Perspective." Unpublished manuscript, Center for Global Development, Washington DC.

Tomich, T. P., M. van Noordwijk, S. A. Vosti, and J. Witcover. 1998. "Agricultural Development with Rainforest Conservation: Methods for Seeking Best Bet Alternatives to Slash-and-Burn, with Applications to Brazil and Indonesia." *Agricultural Economics* 19: 159–74. Reprinted in Hill, H., ed., *The Economic Development of Southeast Asia.* Cheltenham, UK: Edward Elgar Publishing.

UNEP (United Nations Environment Programme). 2006. "Desertification." *Global Resource Information Database.* Washington, DC: UNEP–North America, Division of Early Warning and Assessment. http://www.na.unep.net/des/uncedexsum.php3. Accessed April.

Uphoff, N., A. Ball, E. Fernandes, H. Herren, O. Husson, M. Laing, C. Palm, J. Pretty, P. Sanchez, N. Sanginga, and J. Thies, eds. 2006. *Biological Approaches to Sustainable Soil Systems.* New York: CRC Press.

Vanlauwe, B., J. Diels, K. Aihou, E. N. O. Iwuafor, O. Lyasse, N. Sanginga, and R. Merckx. 2002. "Direct Interactions between N Fertilizer and Organic Matter: Evidence from Trials with ^{15}N-Labelled Fertilizer." In *Integrated Plant Nutrient Management in Sub-Saharan Africa: From Concept to Practice,* ed. B. Vanlauwe et al. Oxon, England: CAB International Wallingford.

Vosti, S., and T. Reardon. 1997. "Introduction: The Critical Triangle of Links among Sustainability, Growth and Poverty Alleviation." In *Sustainability, Growth and Poverty Alleviation: A Policy and Agroecological Perspective,* ed. S. Vosti and T. Reardon, 1–18. Baltimore: Johns Hopkins University Press.

Wood, S. 2005. "Cultivated Systems, Ch. 26." In *Millennium Ecosystem Assessment: Ecosystems and Human Well-being.* Washington, DC: World Resources Institute.

World Bank. 1988. "Renewable Resource Management in Agriculture." Report No. 735. Operations Evaluation Department. World Bank, Washington, DC.

———. 1994. "World Development Report 1994." World Bank, Washington, DC.

———. 1997. *Soil Fertility Initiative.* Washington, DC: World Bank.

———. 2003. *Reaching the Rural Poor: A Renewed Strategy for Rural Development.* Washington, DC: World Bank.

———. 2004. *Agriculture Investment Sourcebook.* Washington, DC: World Bank.

———. 2005. *Shaping the Future of Water for Agriculture: A Sourcebook for Investment in Agricultural Water Management.* Washington, DC: World Bank.

———. 2006a. Carbon Finance Unit Web site. http://www.carbonfinance.org. Accessed April.

———. 2006b. *Reengaging in Agricultural Water Management: Challenges and Options.* Washington, DC: World Bank.

WWF (World Wildlife Federation). 2001. "Integrated Conservation and Development Projects: DGIS-WWF Tropical Forest Portfolio." Workshop Report. WWF International, Gland, Switzerland.

INDEX

Note: Page numbers followed by letters *b, f,* and *t* refer to entries in boxes, figures, and tables, respectively.

A

Africa
  agricultural growth in, 10, 14, 16*b*, 19
  baseline studies in, 70
  climate change in, 24, 25–27, 26*b*
  farmer innovation in, 64
  food production in, 14, 23
  lack of research in, xviii, 61
  land degradation in, 5, 14, 16*b*, 19
  nutrient monitoring in, 61, 62
  nutrient recapitalization in, 37
  sustainable land management in, 32–33, 35, 55*t*, 56, 56*f*, 63, 67
  water management in, 22, 23
African Integrated Land and Water Management Initiative (ALWI), 33
Agriculture. *See also* Land use
  climate change and, 25–27, 26*b*
  pastoral, 27
  rain-fed, 22–24, 25–27, 25*b*, 26*b*, 35, 44

Alternatives to Slash and Burn (ASB) matrix, 60, 60*t*
Asia
  baseline studies in, 49, 70
  food production in, 9–10
  land degradation in, 19
  sustainable land management in, 55*t*, 56*f*, 67
Athi River Mining (ARM), 63

B

Baseline studies, 49, 70–71, 71*f*, 72*f*
BioCarbon Fund, 54, 56*f*
Biodiversity
  conservation of, xvi, 34–35, 45, 48*b*, 49
  measuring, 70–71, 71*f*, 72*f*
Biological nitrogen fixation (BNF) technology, 21
Biosafety, 64
Blue water, 22–23, 23*b*, 24
Brazil, 14, 16*b*, 21, 35, 55*t*, 63, 70
Burkina Faso, 55*t*

C

Cameroon, 70
Carbon funds, xvi, 54–57, 56*f*
Catchment. *See* Watersheds
Catskill Mountains (United States), 39*b*
Cauca Valley (Colombia), 39*b*
Central America
  land degradation in, 5
  soil erosion in, 38, 63
Central Asia, 55*t*
Cerrado zone (Brazil), 14, 16*b*
Certified emissions reduction (CER),
  56
Chile, 66
China, 55*t*
CIMMYT. *See* International Center for
  Maize and Wheat Improvement
Climate change
  adapting to, 24–27
  and agriculture, 2
  effects of, xiv–xv, 3, 25–27, 26*b*
  and poverty, 13
Climate risk management, 24
Common property, xvii, 28–29, 42
Community Development Carbon
  Fund, 54, 56
Consultative Group on International
  Agricultural Research (CGIAR),
  32, 61, 62
Costa Rica, 44

D

Deforestation
  causes of, 13, 19–21, 20*f*
  of hillsides, 6
  impact of, 43–44
  incidence of, 14, 15*f*, 16*b*, 19
Desertification, xiv, 8, 68
Driving Forces, Pressures, State,
  Impacts, Responses (DPSIR), 6–7,
  7*f*

E

East Africa, 10
East Asia, 55*t*, 56*f*, 67
Eastern Europe, 54, 56*f*
Ecosystem services, 5, 6*b*, 14, 27, 33,
  35

Environmental services, 42–49
  payments for, xvi, 33, 44–49, 46*t*–47*t*,
    48*b*
  variety of, 21, 42
Ethiopia, 22
Evaporation, 40*b*
Evapotranspiration, 40*b*, 62–63
Expenditure priorities, xix–xx, 66

F

Farm Input Promotions Africa (FIPS-
  Africa), 63
Farmer innovation, xviii, 63–64
Fertilizer use
  public-private sector partnership
    in, 63
  rainfall and, 22, 37
  risk of, 22
  in soil fertility management, 33,
    35–36, 37
Fiber, 2, 10–11, 13
Financing, xix–xx, 66. *See also*
  Investments
Fisheries, 27
Food
  African production of, 14, 23
  Asian production of, 9–10
  demand for, 10–11
  global production of, 9–10, 9*f*
  global security of, 13
  price of, 9*f*
  requirements for production of, 2
Food and Agriculture Organization
  (FAO), 7, 32, 61
Forests, 43, 43*b*, 53, 54. *See also*
  Deforestation; Reforestation

G

Global Development Learning Network
  (GDLN), 69
Global Environment Facility (GEF),
  xvi, 7, 51, 58, 68–69
Global warming. *See* Climate change
Governments, 13, 31, 51, 65, 66
"Green Revolution," xviii, 61
Green water, 22, 23–24, 23*b*, 44
Groundwater, xvii, 24, 42, 43*b*
Guano, 37

H

Hillside farming, 5–6, 7, 22, 37–39
Humus, 36

I

Incentives
    and land degradation, 3–4, 6, 12, 13
    in sustainable land management,
        xix–xx, 12–13, 29, 38, 44–49, 66
India, 44, 55*t*, 70
Indonesia, 14, 55*t*. *See also* Sumatra
Integrated farming systems, 34–35
Integrated nutrient management, 35,
    36–37
Integrated resource management,
    xv–xvi
International Bank for Reconstruction
    and Development (IBRD), 51–54,
    52*t*, 53*f*
International Center for Maize and
    Wheat Improvement (CIMMYT),
    62
International Development Assistance
    (IDA), 51–54, 52*t*, 53*f*, 69
International Fertilizer Development
    Corporation (IFDC), 32
International Finance Corporation
    (IFC), 51, 66
Investments, 1, 66
    in carbon funds, 54–57, 56*f*
    priorities of, 4
    in research and technology, xvii–xviii
    in water management, 23
Irrigation water, xvii, 22–23, 24, 42, 45

K

Kenya, 61, 63
Knowledge sharing and extension,
    xviii–xix, 27–28, 63–66
Kyoto Protocol, 54, 56

L

Land degradation, xiv, 5–17
    assessment of, xiv, 6–7, 7*f*
    behavioral causes of, 3–4, 6, 12, 13
    causes of, 3–4, 5–6, 10, 14, 19–21,
        20*f*, 27–30
    definition of, 5

effects of, 5, 7, 8–9, 21, 35
    incidence of, 5, 7, 8, 14, 15*f*, 16*b*, 19,
        37–39
    prevention of, xiv, 17
    rehabilitation of, 63
    at watershed level, 8–9
Land Degradation Assessment in
    Drylands, 7
Land use. *See also* Agriculture
    changes in, 10–14, 16, 18
    climate change and, 25–27, 26*b*
    intensification of, xv–xvi, 9–10, 9*f*,
        13–14, 15*f*, 16*b*, 19, 34–35
Landscape, land management at, xiv, 1
Latin America
    agricultural growth in, 14, 16*b*, 19
    baseline studies in, 49, 70
    land degradation in, 14, 16*b*, 19
    sustainable land management in, 55*t*,
        56, 56*f*, 67
Leaching, 36
Legumes, 10, 35, 37

M

Madagascar, 48*b*
Malawi, 30, 62
Mali, 55*t*
Mavuno (fertilizer), 63
Millennium Development Goals, 11
Millennium Ecosystem Assessment
    (MEA), 11, 16–17
Miombo zone (Southern Africa), 14,
    16*b*
Morocco, 55*t*

N

National Action Plans (NAPs), 32, 33,
    68
Natural catastrophes, xiv–xv, 3, 27
Natural resource management (NRM)
    assessment of, 57–58
    investments in, 4
    property rights in, 29–30
Nitrogen, 17, 21, 35, 36–37, 61
North Africa, 55*t*
Nutrient loading, 17
Nutrient recapitalization, 35, 37
Nutrient recycling, 21, 36

Nutrients. *See also* Fertilizer use
combining organic and inorganic,
35, 36, 37
compensating for loss of, 37
enhancing biological sources of, 36–37
research on, 61–62, 63

O

Operations Evaluation Department
(OED), 57–58
Organization for Economic Co-operation
and Development (OECD), 6–7

P

Pastoral agriculture, 27
Payments for environmental services
(PES), xvi, 33, 44–49, 46*t*–47*t*, 48*b*
Peru, 70
Philippines, 13
Phosphorus, 33, 37, 61
Plant functional type (PFT), 70
Policy work
constraints on, 28–30, 65–66
and land degradation, 3–4, 6, 12
in sustainable land management,
xvii, 12, 59–60, 60*t*
Potassium, 61
Poverty
assessment of, 11–12
climate change and, 13
hillside farming and, 5, 37–38
land degradation and, 21, 37–38, 60
and payments for environmental
services, 45, 48*b*
property rights and, 29
water management and, 24
Poverty-reduction strategy program
(PRSP), 50, 68, 69
Property rights, xv, 3–4, 28–30, 64

R

Rainfall, 22, 40*b*
agriculture fed by, 22–24, 25–27, 25*b*,
26*b*, 35, 44
and fertilizer use, 22, 37
Reforestation, 43, 43*b*, 54
Research and technology development,
xvii–xviii, 60–63

Resource sharing, 42
Rift Valley (Kenya), 61
Road building, 21

S

Sector work, xvii, 59–60
Seed research, 62
Soil conservation, 8, 21–22, 32, 38–39,
39*b*
Soil erosion
causes of, 6, 37–38
forests reducing, 43*b*
incidence of, 7
minimizing, 36
rehabilitation of, 63
and sediment load in streams, 24
Soil Fertility Initiative (SFI), 32–33
Soil fertility management, 32–33,
35–37, 61, 62
South Africa, 35
South Asia, 55*t*, 56*f*
Southeast Asia
agricultural growth in, 19
baseline studies in, 49
land degradation in, 5
sustainable land management in, 63
Southern Africa
agricultural growth in, 10, 14, 16*b*
climate change in, 26*b*
Stress-tolerant crops, 63
Sub-Saharan Africa
BioCarbon projects in, 56*f*
climate change in, 26*b*
food production in, 14
nutrient monitoring in, 61
nutrient recapitalization in, 37
soil fertility management in, 33
water management in, 22, 23
Sumatra, 70, 71, 71*f*, 72*f*
Sustainable land management (SLM)
assessment of, 57–58, 69
challenges to, xiv–xv, 18–30
constraints on, 28–30, 65–66
definition of, xiv, 2
examples of successful, 9–10, 9*f*, 13,
21–22, 30, 32, 35
factors for successful, 2–3, 13–14,
34–35, 58

importance of, 13
incentives in, xix–xx, 12–13, 29, 38,
   44–49, 66
information needed for, 67
intervention points in, 6–7, 7*f*, 31–49
investments in. *See* Investments
at landscape level, xiv, 1
objectives of, xiv, 17, 31, 33, 34*b*,
   67–68
opportunities for, xv–xvii, 2
phasing, 67
policy work in, xvii, 12, 59–60, 60*t*
strategic options for, xvii–xx, 12–13,
   29, 59–69
at watershed level, xiv, xvi–xvii, 1,
   39–42, 40*f*, 41*t*, 54, 55*t*
World Bank's portfolio on, 50–58,
   52*t*, 53*f*

T

TerrAfrica, 33
Thailand, 70
Transpiration, 40*b*, 43*b*
Tunisia, 55*t*
Turkey, 55*t*

U

Undernourished people, 9*f*, 11
United Nations Convention to Combat
   Desertification (UNCCD), 68
United Nations Environment Program
   (UNEP), 7

V

V index, 70–71, 71*f*, 72*f*
Vietnam, 13

W

Water, 40*b*
   blue, 22–23, 23*b*, 24
   deforestation and, 43–44
   equitable sharing of, xvi
   green, 22, 23–24, 23*b*, 44
   groundwater, xvii, 24, 42, 43*b*
   for irrigation, xvii, 22–23, 24, 42,
      45
   management of, 22–24, 25*b*, 33, 34*b*,
      35, 41*t*, 42, 62–63
Watersheds
   land management at, xiv, xvi–xvii, 1,
      39–42, 40*f*, 41*t*, 54, 55*t*
   overexploitation of, 8–9
Weeds, 35
West Africa, 10, 62, 63
Working for Water program, 35
World Bank
   African Integrated Land and Water
      Management Initiative of, 33
   Operations Evaluation Department
      of, 57–58
   role of, 67–69
   SLM portfolio of, 50–58, 52*t*,
      53*f*
   Soil Fertility Initiative of, 32
World Bank Institute (WBI), 69